Calendar Quilts

JAN.	FEB.	MAR.	APR.
MAY	JUNE	JULY	AUG.
SEPT.	OCT.	NOV.	DEC.

Joan Hanson

That Patchwork Place®

Credits

Photography . . . . Brent Kane
Illustration and Graphics . . . . Karl St. Pierre
                                             Laurel Strand
Text and Cover Design . . . . Judy Petry
Editors . . . . Liz McGehee
                                             Shellie Tucker

Calendar Quilts©
©1991 by Joan Hanson
That Patchwork Place, Inc.
PO Box 118, Bothell, WA 98041-0118

Printed in the British Crown Colony of Hong Kong
97 96 95 94 93 92 91   6 5 4 3 2 1

Library of Congress Cataloging-in-Publication Data

Hanson, Joan.
    Calendar quilts / Joan Hanson.
        p.   cm.
    ISBN 0-943574-77-3
    1. Machine quilting—Patterns. 2. Patchwork—Patterns.
3. Wall hangings.   I. Title.
TT835.H336 1991
746.46—dc20
                          90-28085
                          CIP

Acknowledgments

I'd first like to thank Mary Hales for saying "Let's do it!" when I came to her and said I'd like to teach a monthly class in her shop. Her continued support and enthusiasm have been wonderful.

Second, I'd like to thank all the women who have come each month to stitch, learn, and laugh. You've made all the washing and cutting worthwhile.

Third, I'd like to thank Nancy J. Martin, who said, "Will you write this up into a book?" I've never thought of myself as an author, but she did.

Fourth, a very special thank you to Janet Kime, who has provided hours of help with the proofing, sketching, spelling, and computerizing of this whole project. Without her this would never have become a book.

My thanks also to Hazel Montague for all of her tiny, even quilting stitches.

Finally a big hug and thank you to Julie Stewart, Pat Thompson, Judy Pollard, Nancy J. Martin, Mary Hickey, Janet Kime, and Cleo Nollette for making "creative alternative" quilts and especially for their steadfast encouragement.

Contents

Introduction

I've always loved working with fabric. As a small child I provided my assorted dolls with complete wardrobes made from leftover scraps. I'm sure this activity kept me busy and out of my mother's hair for hours.

The first quilt I ever made was for my Barbie® doll. It was made from two different fabrics cut into squares and stitched together. I even bound it!

I started making quilts for real in the early 1980s when a wall in my family room needed a large focal point. I wanted a quilt to hang there so I made a six-block sampler in blue and rust. This quilt turned out to be so much fun that I decided to take a beginning quiltmaking class from Marsha McCloskey. By the time the class was over, I was hooked on quilts. Since that first class, I have made many quilts. I do enjoy hand appliqué, but primarily I am drawn to pieced picture blocks or blocks that form a secondary design when put together.

As I became more sophisticated in quiltmaking, I decided to make a wall quilt for each season of the year so I could occasionally change the display in the family room. This idea developed into a quilt for each month of the year when I began teaching a monthly quilt class in a local quilt shop. Now I have completed a quilt for each month of the year, but instead of hanging on my wall they are usually hanging in some quilt shop! Sometimes in August there are Easter bunnies hanging on the wall in my family room.

The quilts in this book were designed to be hung on a wall quilt rack and changed each month of the year. With this in mind, I designed all the quilts to finish to the same width, 36", so they would all fit on the same rack. The lengths of the quilts vary from 40" to 50".

This book evolved out of the classes that I taught over the past two years. Each class contains new techniques, skills or lessons to be learned while making the quilt for that particular month. The quilts begin with basic teaching techniques and progress to more advanced skills so by the end of the year, the beginning quilter will have acquired a thorough quilting background with knowledge of a wide variety of techniques and skills. Lesson Boxes used throughout the book present this information in detail. For best results, read the material in the Lesson Box and experiment with the technique before beginning your quilt. The Lesson Boxes are listed, making it convenient for you to consult the material at any time. I want to thank all the women who came faithfully month after month, sewing machine in hand, to take my class. We learned a lot from each other and had a lot of fun along the way. I was impressed with the variations my students came up with while making

basically the same quilt, by choosing their own border fabric and adding personal embellishments.

I use a variety of sets (such as alternating blocks, diagonal set, medallion set), fabrics (pastels, florals, muted colors, plaids, brights, earth tones, etc.), and techniques so that my students can try new colors and sets. Many students have told me they enjoyed being "stretched" into trying something that they wouldn't have attempted on their own. I hope you are also encouraged to individualize these quilts. A gallery of color photos on pages 9–14 shows most of the quilts in alternate color schemes. Often, changing the color scheme can affect the theme of the quilt, and several of the quilts make ideal baby quilts or gifts. Although these quilts are presented with a seasonal emphasis, don't limit yourself by thinking of them only in that context. Most of the designs offer a great deal of diversity not often found in "beginner quilts."

I have organized this book so it can be used in several different ways:

1. You may begin with the first quilt and continue through each quilt and each lesson. From January to December, the projects start with basic piecing techniques and progress to more advanced techniques. You will pick up new skills with each quilt.
2. The book may be used by an instructor as the basis for a monthly class like the one I teach, in which I prepare kits with the fabric all washed and cut for the students as part of the class fee. Also available is *Calendar Quilts: A Guide to Quantity Cutting* which teaches you how to layer, cut, and kit fabrics. Write Top Teachers Club, PO Box 118, Bothell, WA 98041, for details on this quantity-cutting guide. A registration fee can be charged to cover the price of the book for each student, then a monthly fee to cover the instructor's fee and the cost of the fabric.
3. A quilter with a basic quilting background may choose any quilt, study the Lesson Box, and complete the quilts in any desired order.

However you use the book, I hope you enjoy making these quilts as much as I and my students have. Hardly a month goes by that some student doesn't tell me this month's quilt is her favorite. I hope each quilt you make becomes your favorite as well.

Enjoy!

Getting Started

Basic Sewing Supplies and Equipment

As with any job, having the right tools, supplies, and work space is half the battle. The following list is for guidance only, but even if it takes you some time to accumulate all these items, you will find each one well worth the investment. Several quilts in this book require special tools that aren't listed here. If you plan to add these tools to your collection, add them to this list.

Everyone has tools they just wouldn't be without. Here are my essentials:

Paper Scissors—These are large, sharp scissors that I use to cut everything except fabric, including paper, X-ray film (for plastic templates), and cardboard.

Fabric Scissors—These are my most expensive scissors, and the one pair my kids may not use! They are for fabric only and are so marked.

Embroidery Scissors—You can't have too many pairs of these. I keep a pair at my sewing machine, another at my cutting and ironing table, another in my sewing bag, and still another tied to my chatelaine, hanging around my neck. I use these small scissors for cutting threads and trimming, as well as many other tasks.

Seam Ripper—Again, one is never enough!

Pins—I use the long quilter's pins with glass or plastic heads, and one or two magnetic pin holders. I keep both regular pins and long quilt pins on hand.

Seam Gauge—always comes in handy.

See-through Ruler, 2" x 18"—I use this ruler for drafting templates and other pencil work, not for rotary cutting.

Sewing Machine—A good straight stitch is really all you need. Be sure to have your machine cleaned and oiled regularly as cotton fabric is quite linty. It is important to have a machine that you are comfortable with, one that is your friend and doesn't fight you every step of the way. If you have only a few bobbins for your machine, treat yourself to six or eight more. I wind two or three with a neutral color of thread that I use for many of my projects, so I don't have to stop in the middle of a job to wind bobbins. A can of pressurized air, which can be purchased at fabric stores, is helpful for removing lint from the bobbin area. Blowing the lint away with your mouth adds moisture that attracts more lint.

Rotary Equipment

Cutting Mat—I use one marked with a 1" grid, which I find very helpful in keeping my cuts straight and perpendicular to the fold. The 30" x 36" mat is a good size for cutting large pieces of fabric. If your space is limited or you need a more portable size, an 18" x 24" mat is adequate.

Rotary Cutter—A 2" blade works best for cutting straight lines, and stays sharp longer than smaller blades. When your blade starts to drag and you are tempted to change it, take the cutter apart and clean out the lint that accumulates between the blade and the guard. Put a tiny drop of sewing machine oil on the blade, on the side facing the guard. This simple trick is the next best thing to a new blade!

Acrylic Cutting Guides—These are ⅛"–thick acrylic rulers. The thickness is necessary to guide the rotary blade; if you use a thinner ruler, the blade will roll over the top of the ruler, cutting it and maybe your fingers. There are many types and brands of cutting guides and you may end up owning quite an assortment. I recommend starting with the 6" x 24" cutting guide, the 6" x 6" Bias Square®, and a 15" x 15" square. These three guides, used alone and in combination, will meet most of your needs.

Pressing Equipment

Iron—Buy as good a steam iron as you can afford. The best ones produce lots of steam.

Pressing Pad—Make a portable pad from a cardboard fabric bolt end (ask for one at your quilt shop). Spread a hand towel over it and then pin a piece of fabric over the towel. Keep this pad and an iron right beside your sewing machine for quick pressing between seams.

Plastic Squirt Bottle—Some fabrics need a spray of water in addition to the steam from the iron.

Work Space

Having even a small space to call your own makes it so much easier to work on a project. My work space isn't large, but the space is used very efficiently.

Lighting—Overhead color-corrected fluorescent lighting is at the top of my wish list. Good "task lighting" is also important; gooseneck clamp-on lights are very affordable and give good light right where you need it.

Work Table—My work table is about 30" x 60" and is 36" high so I can comfortably stand while I work. It is covered with plastic laminate and I have made an ironing cover and pad that stay on most of the time. My cutting mat slides on and off the top. There are two wide drawers just below the top for tools, and then a narrow shelf to hold my cutting guides and mats. The rest of the area below I use for stacking baskets to store fabric. I do a lot of work at my table, and have never regretted the cost of having it built.

Work Table

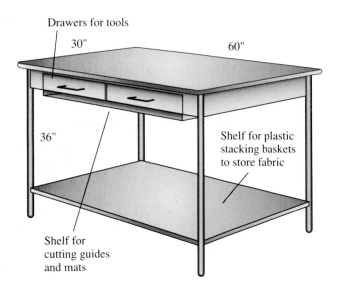

Drawers for tools

30"   60"

36"

Shelf for plastic stacking baskets to store fabric

Shelf for cutting guides and mats

Flannel Board—This is mounted horizontally on wall hooks, but it is easily removed and turned vertically. I made it myself from a 4' x 8' x ½" piece of insulation board, a soft, pressed board that is easy to pin into. I covered the board with a white flannel sheet. I use my board often, to arrange blocks and to squint at my quilts.

Templates

Templates for each quilt have been included for quilters who don't have rotary-cutting equipment. For some odd-shaped pieces, I mount templates on X-ray film or cardboard and carefully cut around them with my rotary cutter. Even if you rotary cut, you may find it helpful to refer to the templates, to visualize the piece as you cut it or to double-check your accuracy.

The following information will help you make optimum use of the templates.

1. The letter designation refers to the piecing diagram for that particular quilt.
2. I have included the name of the quilt on each template. These pieces all start to look the same after a while, so I always label my templates with the name of the quilt pattern.
3. I have also indicated on each template the finished block size. This is just a good habit to get into, since sometimes you will have templates for the same block in a variety of sizes.
4. The number of pieces you need to cut for one block is indicated on each template. The cutting instructions in the text tell how many pieces to cut for the whole quilt.
5. The notation "1 + 1r" indicates that the piece must be reversed for the second cutting.
6. Suggested grain lines are marked on each template. These can be placed on the lengthwise or the crosswise grain.
7. Rotary speed-cutting instructions for each piece are included on the template as well as in the cutting instructions in the text.
8. Many of the triangle templates are drawn both complete and with an indication of where to trim the ends of the points off. Trimming your triangles will help you match the seams more accurately. You may wish to use the templates to trim your triangles, even if you rotary cut.

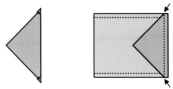

9. Where helpful, both the cut measurements and the finished measurements are indicated.

Rotary Cutting

Rotary-cutting equipment has probably done more for the quilter than anything since the sewing machine came into common use. Speed and accuracy in cutting shapes have been greatly improved. Almost all of the pieces for the quilts in this book were cut using rotary equipment.

Whether you are a newcomer to rotary equipment or have been using it for some time, get in the habit of following a few safety precautions. The rotary blade is extremely sharp and before you notice it you can unintentionally cut something important, like yourself. Develop the habit of pushing the blade guard into place whenever you put your cutter down. If you have small children, keep your cutter safely away from them when not in use.

I use a cutting mat printed with a 1" grid. I find the grid very useful, especially when making my first "cleanup" cut on the raw edges of my fabric. It is critical that this cut be perpendicular to the folded edge, as all other cuts are lined up to this cut edge.

To make a cleanup cut, place your fabric so that the folded edge is lined up on a horizontal grid line at the top of your mat, and the selvage edges are together at the bottom of your mat.

Line up the acrylic ruler (a 6" x 24" one works best) so that all layers of the raw edges are just covered and the lines of your ruler match up with the vertical grid of your mat. Start cutting at the selvages and cut to the fold at the top, so the blade is moving away from you.

As you make additional cuts, line up your ruler with the cut edge of the fabric. Use the grid on your mat to double-check that you are making accurate cuts.

Mastering the
¼" Seam Allowance

Once you have cut your pieces accurately, the next step to master is the ¼" seam allowance. Some blocks have many seams in them; if your ¼" seam allowance is just a little off, the error is multiplied by the number of seams, and this can really add up. I like to stitch just shy of ¼", because when the seam is pressed to one side there is some fabric taken up in the fold.

The key here is some method of marking your sewing machine so that you can line up the edge of your fabric and stitch a consistent ¼" from the edge. Never trust the markings on your sewing machine without first checking them against a Bias Square® or ¼" graph paper. If you can move the needle position on your machine from left to right, move it as far as it will go to the right. This allows the feed dog to pull evenly on the fabric, and the fabric feeds through straighter. Next, take your Bias Square and drop your needle down just to the right of the ¼" line, with the base of the Bias Square lined up with the base of your machine.

Now mark this line with several layers of ¼" masking tape, or opt for my favorite material and use a small strip of Dr. Scholl's® Foot and Shoe Padding. This is ⅛" thick foam rubber with a sticky backing. Cut several ¼" x 1" pieces (I cut several at a time so I have replacements on hand) and attach one to your sewing machine as a ¼" seam guide. The padding provides a nice high ridge to guide your fabric along. It can be removed when you need to sew wider seams and reused until it isn't sticky anymore.

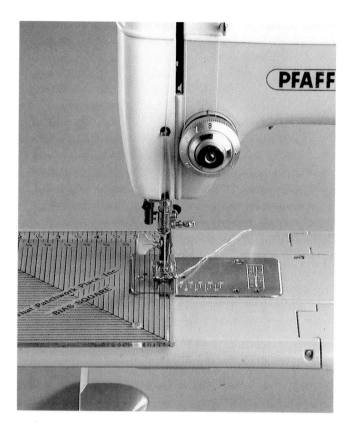

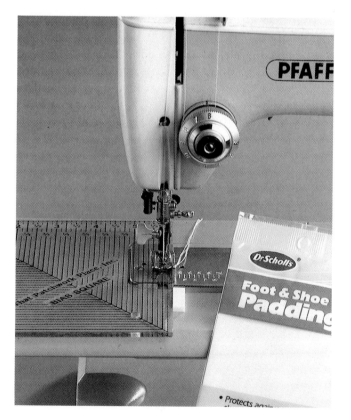

Gallery of Quilts

Victorian Valentines (February) by Joan Hanson, 1990, Seattle, Washington, 36" x 48". The wonderful border fabric inspired the colors used in this romantic quilt. The hearts were hand appliquéd with the lace added at the same time and stuffed from the back with heart-shaped batting.

Sweet Talk (February) by Cleo Nollette, 1990, Seattle, Washington, 36" x 48". This red and white quilt, with accents of other primary colors, would warm a heart any day of the year.

Autumn Vintage *(October) by Judy Pollard, 1990, Seattle, Washington, 36" x 46". Grapes warming in the fall sun were the inspiration for this quilt.*

Falling Leaves *(October) by Joan Hanson, 1989, Seattle, Washington, 36" x 46". Leaves changing color create the feeling of autumn.*

Beach Ball Buddies *(August) by Julie Stewart, 1990, Bothell, Washington, 36" x 48". By limiting the colors to blue and yellow, this quilt takes on a different look.*

Handkerchief Baskets *(May) by Nancy J. Martin, 1990, Woodinville, Washington, 33" x 47". The center of each cheerful yellow basket in this quilt has been cut from the corners of floral handkerchiefs that belonged to Nancy's grandmother.*

Schoolmates *(September) by Chikako Nichols, 1990, Mukilteo, Washington, 36" x 48". Happy children of the world hold hands across the school yard.*

Quiet Traditions *(September) by Lauren Turpen, 1990, Seattle, Washington, 36" x 48". This quilt commemorates the traditions and values that are carried forth by several generations of families at Holy Rosary School in West Seattle.*

Colonial Bunnies *(April) by Mary Hickey, 1990, Seattle, Washington, 36" x 46". These charming plaid and striped bunnies would feel right at home in a little boy's room.*

Our First German Christmas *(December) by Pat Thompson, 1990, Duisburg, Germany, 36" x 48". This quilt was made in honor of the quiltmaker's first Christmas in Germany.*

Night Blooms (March) by Janet Kime, 1990, Vashon Island, Washington, 36" x 48". Jewel tones on black make a vibrant wall hanging.

Happy Father's Day, Daddy (June) by Janet Kime, 1990, Vashon Island, Washington, 36" x 40". Shirts and ties that only a daddy would wear.

Quilt Patterns
and
Lessons

January: Snowball

Lessons
Chain Piecing
Pressing

The overall design of this quilt is created by alternating two very simple blocks, Ninepatch and Snowball. The blue and white fabrics remind me of a crisp winter day.

Quilt size: 36" x 48"
Block size: 6" (finished)
Number of blocks: 18 Ninepatch blocks and 17 Snowball blocks

Fabric Required for Quilt Top
1½ yds. total of medium blue to dark blue fabrics, about 10–20 different fabrics, any combination of prints, solids, stripes, dots, plaids, and the like
¾ yd. white background
½ yd. blue border fabric

Cutting Instructions

Medium and Dark Blues
1. Cut a total of 162 squares 2½" x 2½" from a variety of fabrics, using either rotary-cutting equipment or Template A.
2. Cut a total of 34 squares 2⅞" x 2⅞" from a variety of fabrics. Cut each square in half diagonally to make 68 triangles; cut off corners of triangles using Template C. OR, cut 68 triangles using Template C.

Background
Cut 17 squares 6½" x 6½". Using the corners-cut-off Template D, cut the 4 corners off each square to make an octagon. (Discard the little triangles, or save them for another project.) OR, cut 17 octagons using Template B.

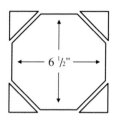

Border
Cut 4 strips of the border fabric, each 3½" x 42".

Piecing Instructions

Ninepatch Blocks

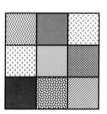

1. Sew 3 blue squares, 2½" x 2½", together to make a row. Select the fabrics randomly.

For each Ninepatch block, you will need 3 rows; to make 18 Ninepatch blocks, you will need a total of 54 rows. A speedy way to assemble the Ninepatch blocks is to chain piece them. (See Chain Piecing in the Lesson Boxes for instructions.)

Keep going until you have 54

2. Add a third square to each of your 54 pairs, again chain piecing.

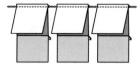

***Snowball** (January) by Joan Hanson, 1989, Seattle, Washington, 36" x 48". The medium and dark blue scraps along with the white Snowball block give this quilt a crisp look. The monochromatic color scheme and simple-to-piece blocks make it a good choice for a beginning project.*

Lesson Boxes—January

Chain Piecing

Chain piecing is a speedy way to machine sew a series of seams. As you sew, don't stop and cut the threads between each seam. Feed in the pieces end-to-end and sew all the seams, then stop and snip the threads between pieces.

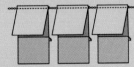

Pressing

In machine piecing, each seam should be pressed before it is crossed with another seam. Press each seam from the wrong side of the fabric, then turn the piece over and press from the right side. Push the side of the iron into the bump of the seam, eliminating any pleats and pressing the piece flat.

Pressing directions have been included for many of the quilts in this book. If you press seam allowances in the directions indicated, you will find that the seam allowances at many intersections are pressed in opposite directions. This evenly distributes the seam allowances' bulk. Also, since the seam allowances butt against each other, it is easier to match seam lines at the intersection and to sew the seam accurately

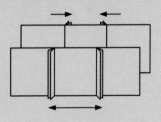

3. Count out 18 rows into a stack. Press the seams in this stack toward the center square. (For hints on pressing, see Pressing in the Lesson Boxes.)

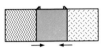

4. Press the seams of the other rows toward the outside.

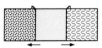

5. Complete the Ninepatch block by sewing the 3 rows together. Again, chain piece: sew 18 pairs of rows together, then sew on the third row.

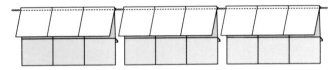

6. Press the final seams toward the center row.

Snowball Blocks

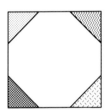

1. Seam 4 blue corner triangles to each white center. Select the triangles randomly so the snowballs have a "scrappy" look. If you trim the corners off the triangles with Template C before sewing them to the octagon, you can match the edges for a more accurate seam.

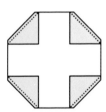

2. Press the seams toward the blue corners.

Assembling the Quilt

1. Alternating Ninepatch blocks with Snowball blocks, lay 7 rows of 5 blocks each. Move the blocks around to achieve a good distribution of the different fabrics. If there are a few fabrics that especially stand out, sprinkle them around the quilt rather than allowing them to collect in one area.

2. Sew the blocks into 7 rows. Press the seams toward the Ninepatch blocks.

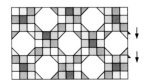

3. Sew the rows together. Press these seams all in the same direction.

4. Trim off the selvages from the 4 border strips.
5. Sew the side borders on first, then the top and bottom borders. For more detailed instructions on adding borders, see the chapter on Finishing, page 93.

Quilting Suggestions

Quilt diagonal lines through the centers of the Ninepatch blocks.

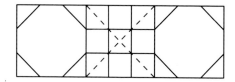

In each white snowball, quilt a snowflake. One design that could be quilted in each block is shown on Template B—or you could draw 17 different snowflakes so that no 2 are alike.

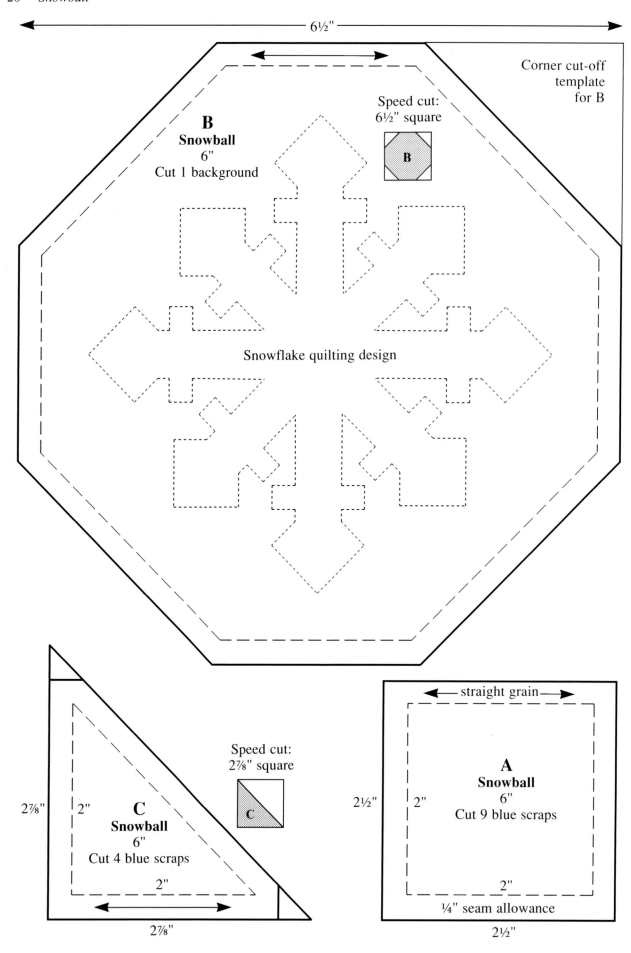

6½"

B
Snowball
6"
Cut 1 background

Speed cut:
6½" square

B

Corner cut-off
template
for B

Snowflake quilting design

2⅞"

2"

C
Snowball
6"
Cut 4 blue scraps

2"

2⅞"

Speed cut:
2⅞" square

C

straight grain

2½"

2"

A
Snowball
6"
Cut 9 blue scraps

2"

¼" seam allowance

2½"

February: Cross My Heart

Lessons
Freezer-Paper Appliqué
Wonder-Under™ and Blanket-Stitch Appliqué

The arrow block is a quick block to piece with very few points to match up. If you choose to make all the arrows red, be sure to vary the color and visual texture of your fabrics enough so that the arrows are distinct from each other and the points don't run together. For fun, you can embroider Valentine candy sayings onto the hearts (instructions provided on page 23).

Quilt size: 36" x 48"
Block size: 6" (finished)
Number of blocks: 24 arrow blocks

Fabric Required for Quilt Top
1¼ yds. background (includes fabric for inner border)
¼ yd. each of 12 fabrics for arrows (or use scraps)
¼ yd. solid red for appliqué hearts
½ yd. red fabric for outer border

Cutting Instructions

Background
1. Cut 4 strips for the inner border from the lengthwise grain of the fabric (parallel to the selvage): cut 2 strips 3" x 37", and 2 strips 3" x 31".
2. Cut 24 squares 5½" x 5½". Cut the squares in half diagonally, and then use Template A to trim the corners. OR, cut 48 of Template A.

Arrow Fabrics
From each of the 12 arrow fabrics, cut 2 rectangles 2½" x 4¾", and 2 squares 3⅞" x 3⅞". Cut each of the squares in half diagonally to make 2 triangles. Use Template C to trim the corners. OR, from each of the arrow fabrics, cut 2 of Template B and 4 of Template C.

Solid Red
Directions for cutting the hearts are provided with the appliqué directions on page 23.

Border
From outer border fabric, cut 4 strips, each 4" x 43".

Piecing Instructions

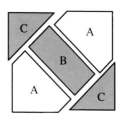

1. Referring to piecing diagram, add background pieces A to both sides of the rectangle of arrow fabric B. Press seams toward B.

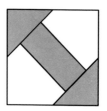

2. Add triangles C, of the same arrow fabric as rectangle B, to each end. Press seams toward the triangles.

Assembling the Quilt
1. Lay out the arrow blocks as shown in the diagram, so that the arrows point as shown and the different fabrics are well distributed.

Cross My Heart *(February) by Joan Hanson, 1989, Seattle, Washington, 36" x 48".*
A soft background that appears tea-dyed and muted reds and pinks give this
Valentine quilt an old-time look. Quilted by an anonymous Amish quilter.

2. Sew the arrows into 6 rows of 4 arrow blocks each. Press the seams in the top row all in the same direction, and press the seams in the second row in the opposite direction. Continue, pressing seams in opposite directions down through the rows.

3. Sew the rows together. Press these seams all in the same direction

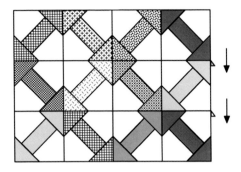

4. Appliqué the hearts (see directions on this page).

5. Add the border strips. Add the 4 background strips first for an inner border, then the 4 wider strips of outer border fabric. For detailed instructions, see Adding Borders, page 93.

Appliquéing the Hearts

Before you appliqué the hearts to the quilt, you may want to embroider on Valentine candy-heart sayings. Some suggestions:

MY GUY	NEXT TIME	BE MINE
SO-SO	LET'S KISS	MY TURN
WHY NOT?	TRUE LOVE	HOT STUFF
HUG ME	I DO	LOVE YOU

Choose either the freezer-paper method or the Wonder-Under™ method to appliqué your hearts. (See the Lesson Boxes for instructions.)

If you plan to use the freezer-paper appliqué technique, cut 8 hearts using Template D. Add ¼" seam allowance as you cut out the hearts. Follow the directions in the Lesson Box for freezer-paper appliqué to prepare the hearts.

If you plan to use Wonder-Under, trace Template D onto the smooth side of the Wonder-Under. Cut out, cutting a little outside the drawn line. Fold each heart in half and cut a heart from the center, leaving about ¼" from your cut to the drawn heart.

Press the rough side of the Wonder-Under heart to the solid red heart fabric. You do not need to leave any seam allowance around the hearts. Cut out the heart shapes on the drawn lines. Remove the paper backing and press in place wherever 4 arrow blocks meet.

continued on pp. 25

Lesson Boxes—February

Freezer-Paper Appliqué

1. For each piece, trace your design onto freezer paper and cut it out. Do not add a seam allowance.
2. Press the freezer paper onto the wrong side of your fabric with the shiny side of the paper toward the fabric, leaving a ¼" space around each piece.
3. Cut out the pieces, adding a ¼" seam allowance around each piece.

4. Turn the seam allowance under and baste it down, sewing through the freezer paper. Baste carefully around curves, easing in the fullness and taking fairly small stitches so the curve is smooth.

5. Fold the seam allowance around both sides of each heart point, first one side and then the other. Baste in place.

6. Clip and baste carefully around inside curves and inside point of each heart. When you draw near an inside point, clip the crevice once almost to the freezer paper. Baste both sides down securely.

7. After the piece is basted, press it lightly.
8. Pin the piece in place on your design. Appliqué it down, starting and stopping on a straight area or a gentle curve. Use thread to match the fabric you are appliquéing to (red, in the Cross My Heart quilt), not the background fabric.

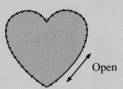

To appliqué almost invisibly, bring the needle up through just a few threads right in the fold of the seam allowance. Push the needle back down in virtually the same spot. Bring the needle back up ⅛"–¼" over, and again catch just a few threads in the fold of the seam allowance. If you stitch in this way, there is only a tiny stitch on the surface; most of the stitch is on the wrong side of the block.

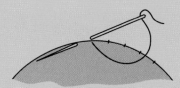

9. Stitch all around the piece, leaving a 1" opening. When you reach the stopping place, remove the basting threads. Reach in and loosen the freezer paper, and pull it out. You can do this with your fingers or a pair of tweezers (scissor-handled ones are nice). If you use tweezers, reach in and grab the freezer paper, rotate the tweezers to curl the paper around them, and pull the paper out.

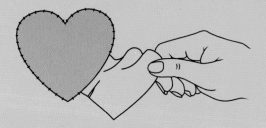

10. Continue appliquéing, stitching the opening down.

Wonder-Under™ and Blanket-Stitch Appliqué

1. Trace your design on the smooth side of Wonder-Under™ and cut it out on the drawn line. Do not add a seam allowance.

2. Press the rough side of the Wonder-Under shape to your fabric. Cut out the shape on the drawn line.

3. Peel the paper from the Wonder-Under. Lay the piece in place on your background fabric, Wonder-Under side down, and press with your iron.

4. With 2 strands of contrasting embroidery floss, sew the piece down around the edges with a blanket stitch.

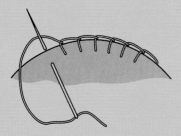

The hearts are appliquéd wherever 4 arrow blocks meet. Pin the hearts in place. If you are using the freezer-paper method, appliqué each heart with red thread. If you are using the Wonder-Under method, blanket stitch around each heart with contrasting embroidery floss.

Quilting Suggestions

Outline the arrows and hearts by quilting around them. Stitch on whichever side of the arrows does not have a seam allowance as shown below.

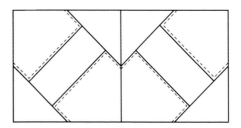

Quilt hearts and arrows in the border.

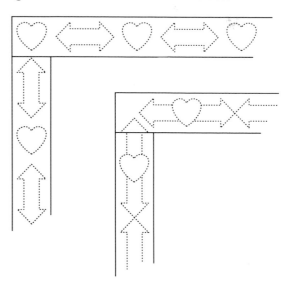

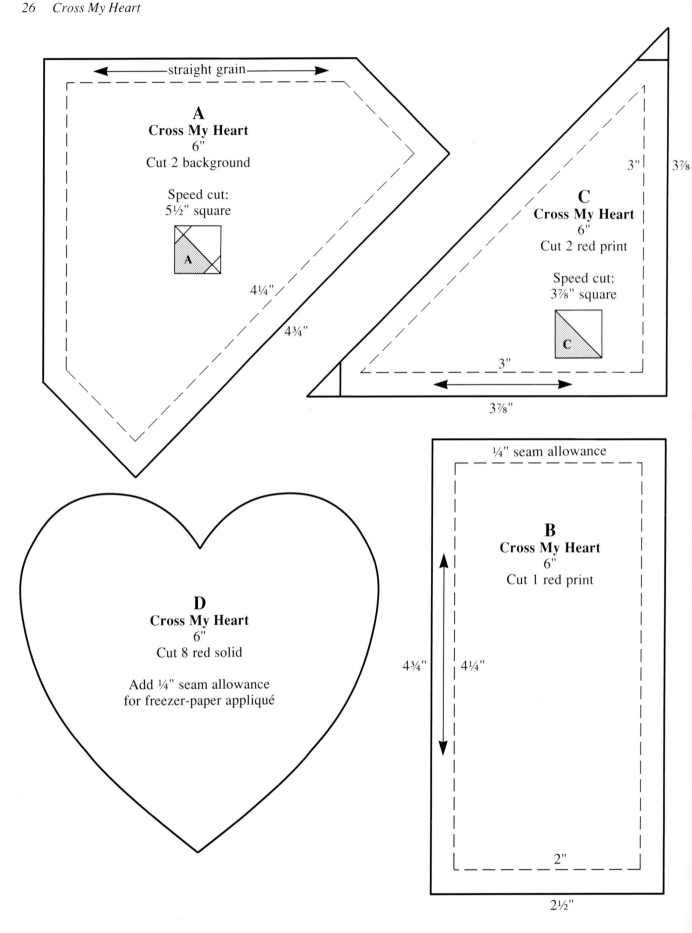

straight grain

A
Cross My Heart
6"
Cut 2 background

Speed cut:
5½" square

4¼"

4¾"

3"

3⅞"

C
Cross My Heart
6"
Cut 2 red print

Speed cut:
3⅞" square

3"

3⅞"

D
Cross My Heart
6"
Cut 8 red solid

Add ¼" seam allowance
for freezer-paper appliqué

¼" seam allowance

B
Cross My Heart
6"
Cut 1 red print

4¾"   4¼"

2"

2½"

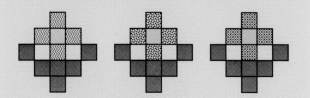

March: Irish Rose

Lesson
Strip Piecing

This cross-stitch-like design is reminiscent of quilts made by Anne Orr, the well-known 1930s quilt designer and needlework editor. The Fall/Winter 1983 edition of *Quiltmaker* magazine, which featured a quilt called "Irish Jig" by Susie Ennis and Judy Martin, gave me my inspiration.

Sashing strips and set squares are easy to assemble using strip-piecing techniques, and they add much liveliness to this springlike flower block. Repeating the flower colors in the binding gives a colorful finishing touch to the quilt.

Be sure to choose a soft green and strong flower colors so that the green doesn't dominate the flowers.

Quilt size: 36" x 48"
Block size: 7½" (finished)
Number of blocks: 6 flower blocks

Fabric Required for Quilt Top
1¼ yds. light background
1 yd. green fabric
⅛ yd. yellow for flower centers
⅛ yd. each of 6 flower colors

Cutting Instructions
The Irish Rose quilt is largely strip pieced, so it goes together quite quickly. If you are new to rotary cutting, refer to the section on rotary-cutting basics, page 7. Although templates are provided so it is not necessary to rotary cut, this is a good project on which to learn rotary-cutting techniques.

Background
1. Make 17 cuts 2" wide; from 2 of these cuts plus part of another, make 48 squares 2" x 2". OR, cut 48 of Template A.
2. Make 2 cuts 3½" wide; trim each to 26" long.

Green
1. Make 9 cuts 2" wide; make 6 pieces 2" x 5" from part of 1 cut; trim 1 other cut to 26". OR, cut 6 of Template C and 1 strip 2" x 26".
2. Make 4 cuts 3¼" wide for the border.

Yellow
Make 1 cut 2" wide; make 6 squares 2" x 2". OR, cut 6 of Template A.

Flower Colors
Make 1 cut 2" wide of each of 6 colors; from each color, make 6 squares 2" x 2". OR, cut 6 of Template A from each of 6 colors.

Piecing Instructions
See the Lesson Box for strip-piecing instructions.

Sashing Strips
1. Take eight 2" cuts of background fabric and four 2" cuts of green.
2. Sew a background cut to each side of the 4 green cuts, as illustrated. Press the seams toward the green fabric.
3. From the sets of strips in step 2, cut 17 crosscuts, each 8" wide.

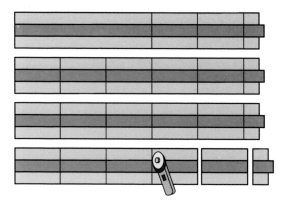

4. From the leftovers, cut 6 crosscuts, each 2" wide, and set these aside for the bottom stem section of the flower blocks.

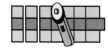

Irish Rose *(March) by Joan Hanson, 1989, Seattle, Washington, 36" x 48". Welcome*
spring with fresh flowers pieced into this quick strip-pieced quilt.
Quilted by an anonymous Amish quilter.

Flower Blocks

1. Sew a 3½" background cut to each side of a 2" green cut, as illustrated below. Press seams toward the green fabric.
2. Make 12 crosscuts, each 2" wide, and set aside.

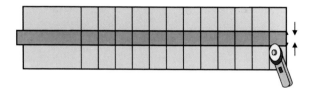

3. Assemble the Ninepatch section of the flower block. For each flower color, make 2 rows of 3 squares each of background plus flower color plus background. Press seams toward flower fabrics.

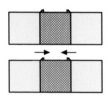

4. For each flower color, make 1 row of 3 squares of flower plus yellow plus flower. Press seams toward the flower fabrics.

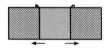

5. For each color, sew the 3 rows together into a Ninepatch block. You should have 6 Ninepatch blocks.

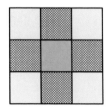

6. Make 6 flower stems, sewing the 5" pieces of green (Template C) to the 2" crosscuts left over from the sashing strips. Press seams toward the green rectangles.

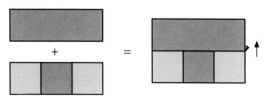

7. Sew the flower stems to the flowers. Press seams toward the stems.

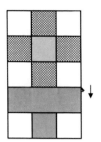

8. Sew a long crosscut from steps 1 and 2 to each side of the flower. Press seams toward the crosscuts.

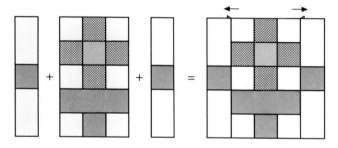

Set Squares

1. Piece 2" cuts to make 2 green cuts 50" long and 1 background cut 50" long.
2. Sew the green cuts to either side of the background cut. Press seams toward the green.
3. Make 24 crosscuts, each 2" wide.

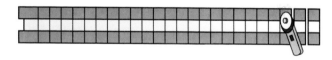

4. Take 24 squares 2" x 2" of background fabric and the 12 remaining 2" squares of the flower colors. Sew 2 background squares to each flower square, as shown. Press seams toward the flower fabrics.

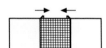

5. Assemble the strips into the set-square Ninepatch blocks.

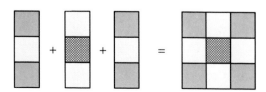

Lesson Box—March

Strip Piecing

Strip piecing involves 4 basic steps:

1. Fabrics are cut into strips 44" long (selvage to selvage). Each of these strips is called a "cut."
2. The strips are sewn to each other lengthwise to make 2 "strip units."

Strip unit →

3. The strip units are cut crosswise into new strips, each of which is composed of several fabrics. These crosswise strips are called "crosscuts."

Cross cut

4. The crosscuts are assembled into blocks.

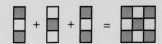

Many quilt designs can be broken down into parts that can be strip pieced. The simplest ones are those in which strips of the same width are sewn into a strip unit, which is then crosscut into equal-width pieces. A wide variety of patterns can be formed from variations on this technique; an example is Homespun Spools (November, page 80), in which a 2-cut strip unit is crosscut at a 45° angle. As you look at quilt designs, look for segments that can be strip pieced. You'll find it more accurate and efficient to stitch before you cut!

Assembling the Quilt

1. Arrange the flower blocks, sashing strips, and set squares as shown. Sew the rows together and press all seams toward the sashing strips.

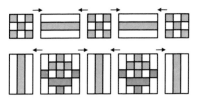

2. Sew the rows to each other and press the seams all in the same direction.

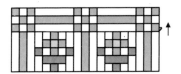

3. You should have 4 of the 2" cuts of background fabric left. Sew 2 strips to the sides of the quilt, and the other 2 strips to the top and bottom. See Adding Borders, page 93, for detailed instructions.
4. Add the 4 strips of green border fabric in the same manner, pressing seams toward the green fabric.

A colorful binding can be made from the leftover flower strips. For instructions see Binding Your Quilt, pages 94–95.

Quilting Suggestions

Quilt in diagonal lines.

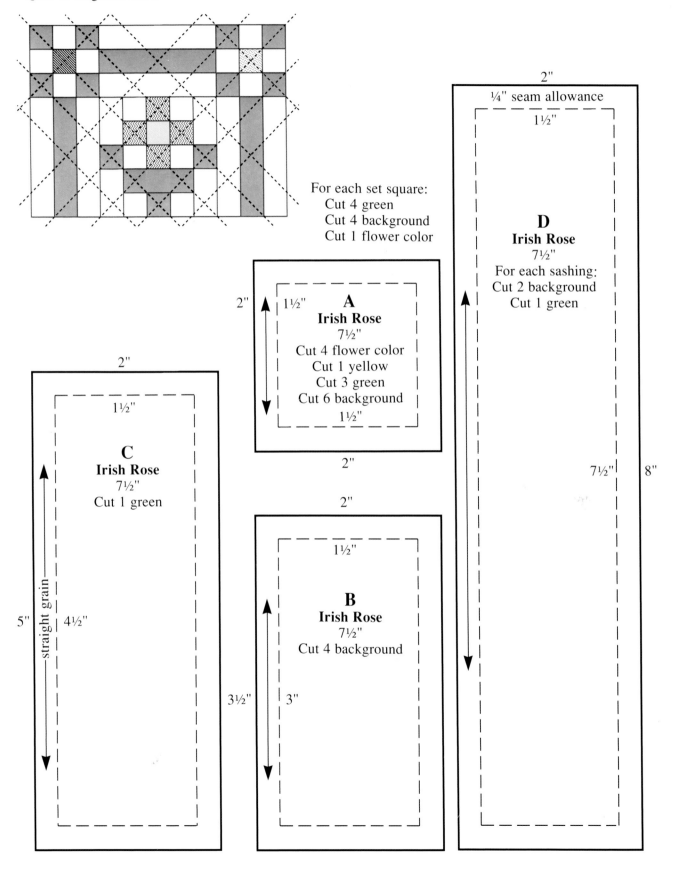

For each set square:
  Cut 4 green
  Cut 4 background
  Cut 1 flower color

2"

¼" seam allowance

1½"

D
Irish Rose
7½"
For each sashing:
Cut 2 background
Cut 1 green

7½"   8"

2"

1½"

A
Irish Rose
7½"
Cut 4 flower color
Cut 1 yellow
Cut 3 green
Cut 6 background

1½"

2"   2"

2"   2"

1½"

B
Irish Rose
7½"
Cut 4 background

3½"   3"

1½"

C
Irish Rose
7½"
Cut 1 green

straight grain

5"   4½"

April: Bunny Trail

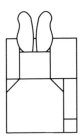

Lesson
Sewing and Turning Small Shapes

With their ears going every which way, each bunny in Bunny Trail takes on its own personality. This design would make a charming baby quilt for a lucky little one.

Quilt size: 36" x 46"
Block size: Bunny, 8" x 10½" (finished)
         Carrot, 3" x 10½" (finished)
Number of blocks: 9 bunny blocks and 3 carrot blocks

Fabric Required for Quilt Top
¼ yd. each of 9 bunny colors
1 yd. background
⅛ yd. orange for carrots
⅛ yd. green for carrots
½ yd. for trails (horizontal sashing strips)
½ yd. outer border fabric

Cutting Instructions

Bunny Fabric (cut the following from each fabric)
1. Cut 1 piece 5" x 10" for ears.
2. Cut 1 piece 3½" x 4" (Template B) for head.
3. Cut 1 piece 6½" x 7", and use corner cut-off on Template D to trim off corners for body.
4. Cut 1 square 2" x 2" (Template F) for tail.

Background
1. Cut 9 pieces 2" x 4" (Template C).
2. Cut 9 squares 2⅜" x 2⅜", then cut them in half diagonally to make 18 triangles. OR, cut 18 of Template E.
3. Cut 18 pieces 2" x 5" (Template G).
4. Cut 9 pieces 3½" x 5" (Template H).
5. Cut 6 of Template J.
6. Cut 6 of Template L.

7. Cut 3 pieces 2" x 3½" (Template M).
8. Cut 4 strips 2" x 44" (that is, cut 2" strips the width of the fabric).

Carrot Orange
Cut 3 of Template I.

Carrot Green
Cut 3 of Template K.

Trail Sashing
Cut 3 strips 2" x 28".

Outer Border
Cut 4 strips 4" x 44" (that is, cut 4" strips the width of the fabric).

Piecing Instructions

Bunny Blocks

1. To make the ears, fold the 5" x 10" piece of bunny fabric in half crosswise, right sides together.
2. Trace the bunny ear pattern (Template A) twice on the folded fabric, leaving ¼" between the ears. Do not cut the ears out yet!
3. Stitch around each ear, leaving the bottoms open.

Leave open

4. Cut out each ear, leaving a ⅛" seam allowance. Turn right side out and press.
5. Make a ¼" tuck in the bottom of each ear.
6. Pin the ears to the top of Template B, matching raw edges, with the straight side of the ears toward the center and the ears pointing down. If you choose to use a different fabric for the lining of the ears, make sure the lining fabric faces the right side of head piece (Template B).

Bunny Trail *(April) by Joan Hanson, 1989, Seattle, Washington, 36" x 46". Each of these floppy-eared bunnies takes on its own delightful personality as it hops down the bunny trail.*

Lesson Box—April

Sewing and Turning Small Shapes

A ¼" seam allowance can be too bulky for small piecing projects, especially pieces that are turned right side out as the bunny ears are. A narrower seam allowance is difficult to manage on a sewing machine.

A great solution is to draw your shapes with templates that do not include a seam allowance. Leave ¼" between shapes. Sew your seams on the drawn lines. To get a nice smooth curve, shorten your stitch length to about 12–14 stitches to the inch. As you go around the curve, raise and lower your presser foot every few stitches to allow the fabric to make the turn.

Cut out shapes, adding only ⅛" seam allowance; turn.

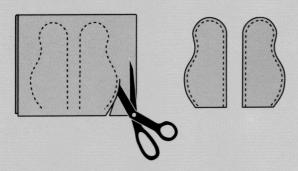

When pressing, insert a wooden popsicle stick and push it into the curve as you press to make a smooth edge without any pleats.

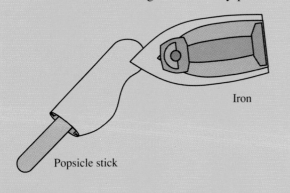

Iron

Popsicle stick

7. Place background piece (Template C) on the seam, right sides together, and stitch, sewing the ears into the seam.

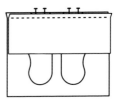

8. Continue piecing the bunny block as shown. Sew both E's to D, and sew F to 1 of the G's before assembling. Be sure to make both left-tailed bunnies and right-tailed bunnies by reversing pieces F, G, and H. Press.

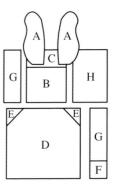

Carrot Blocks

1. Referring to piecing diagram, sew background pieces (Template J) to the sides of the orange carrot (Template I). Press seams toward the carrot.
2. Sew background pieces (Template L) to the sides of the green carrot top (Template K). Press seams toward the green.
3. Assemble carrot block as shown.

Assembling the Quilt

1. Arrange the carrot and bunny blocks into 3 rows, as shown. Seam together. Press seams all in the same direction.

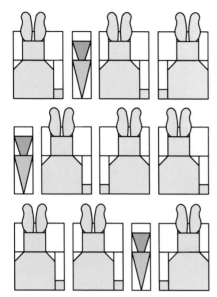

2. Add the trail sashing strips to the bottom of each row. Press the seams toward the sashing strips. Trim the ends.

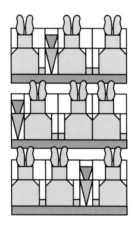

3. Sew the 3 bunny rows to each other.
4. Add a strip of background 2" x 44" to each side, press seams toward background, and trim the ends.
5. Add a strip of background 2" x 44" to the top and to the bottom, press the seams toward the background, and trim the ends.
6. Repeat steps 4 and 5 with the outer border fabric. (See Adding Borders, page 93, for detailed instructions.)
7. Embroider the bunnies' faces, or combine embroidery and button eyes, or draw the faces with a Pilot SC-UF permanent pen (see Template B).

Quilting Suggestions

Stitch in the ditch around the bunnies and carrots. Quilt a heart on each bunny as shown on Template D. Quilt the background and border in diagonal lines 2" apart as shown below.

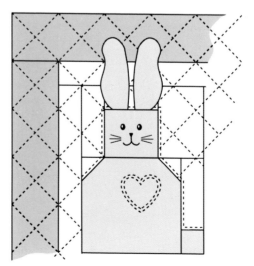

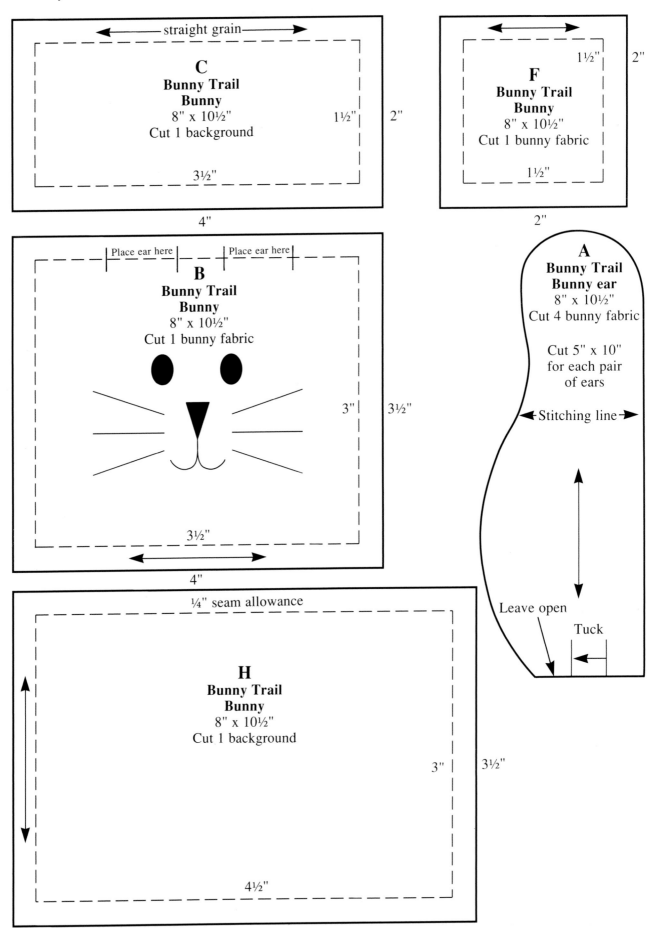

C
Bunny Trail
Bunny
8" x 10½"
Cut 1 background

straight grain

1½"
2"
3½"
4"

F
Bunny Trail
Bunny
8" x 10½"
Cut 1 bunny fabric

1½"
2"
1½"
2"

B
Bunny Trail
Bunny
8" x 10½"
Cut 1 bunny fabric

Place ear here   Place ear here

3"
3½"
3½"
4"

A
Bunny Trail
Bunny ear
8" x 10½"
Cut 4 bunny fabric

Cut 5" x 10"
for each pair
of ears

Stitching line

Leave open

Tuck

H
Bunny Trail
Bunny
8" x 10½"
Cut 1 background

¼" seam allowance

3"
3½"
4½"
5"

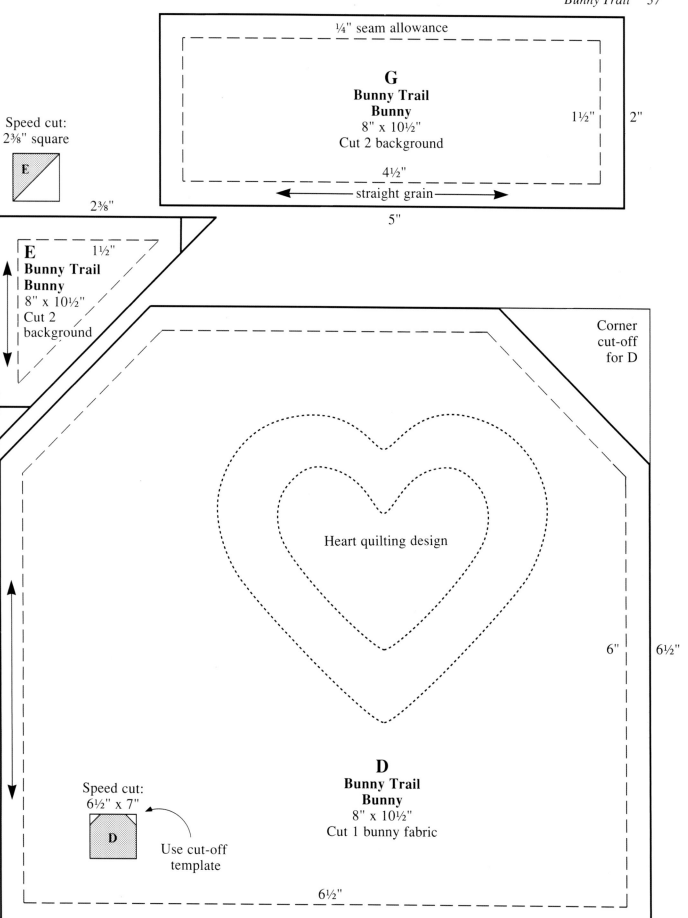

¼" seam allowance

G
Bunny Trail
Bunny
8" x 10½"
Cut 2 background

1½"

2"

4½"

straight grain

5"

Speed cut:
2⅜" square

E

2⅜"

E
Bunny Trail
Bunny
8" x 10½"
Cut 2
background

1½"

Corner
cut-off
for D

Heart quilting design

6"

6½"

D
Bunny Trail
Bunny
8" x 10½"
Cut 1 bunny fabric

Speed cut:
6½" x 7"

D

Use cut-off
template

6½"

7"

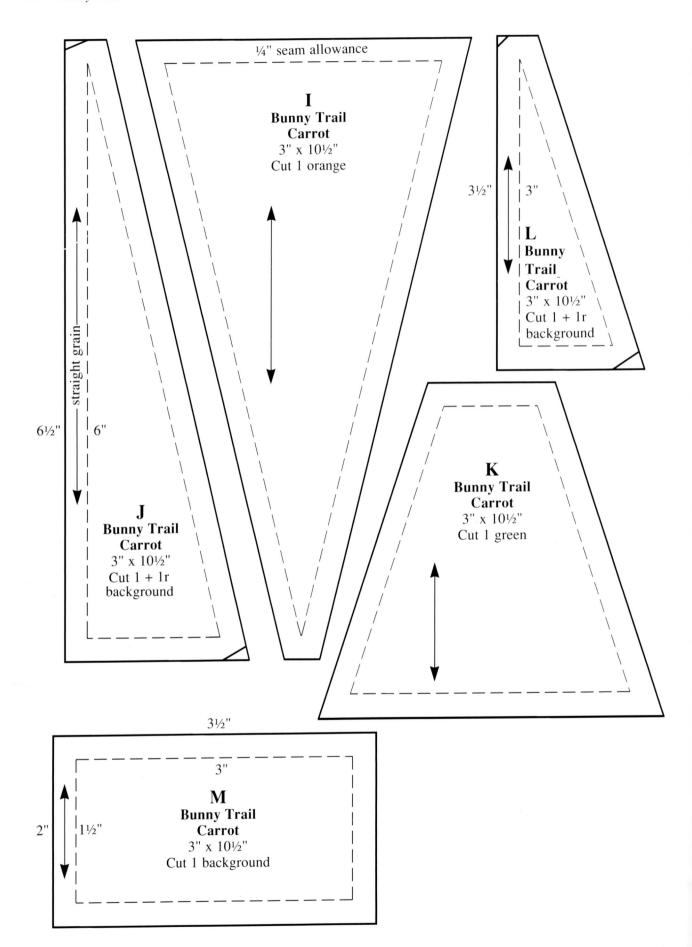

¼" seam allowance

I
Bunny Trail
Carrot
3" x 10½"
Cut 1 orange

3½"   3"

L
Bunny Trail Carrot
3" x 10½"
Cut 1 + 1r background

straight grain

6½"   6"

J
Bunny Trail
Carrot
3" x 10½"
Cut 1 + 1r background

K
Bunny Trail Carrot
3" x 10½"
Cut 1 green

3½"

3"

M
Bunny Trail
Carrot
3" x 10½"
Cut 1 background

2"   1½"

May: May Baskets

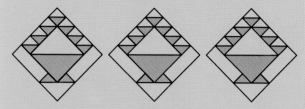

Lessons
**Speed Piecing Triangles with the Bias Square®
Diagonal Sets**

These simple baskets float on a lovely chintz background. Choose a floral background fabric with a variety of colors, and select solid-color basket fabrics to coordinate with the background.

Quilt size: 36" x 50"
Block size: 10" (finished)
Number of blocks: 6 Basket blocks and 2 plain blocks

Fabric Required for Quilt Top
1¼ yds. plain background
½ yd. each of 6 solid-color fabrics for baskets
⅞ yd. floral print
½ yd. border fabric

Cutting Instructions

Background
1. Cut 3 squares 6⅞" x 6⅞" (Template B), then cut them in half diagonally to make 6 triangles.
2. Cut 3 squares 4⅞" x 4⅞" (Template D), then cut them in half diagonally to make 6 triangles.
3. Cut 12 rectangles 2½" x 6½" (Template C).
4. Cut a 13" strip 44" wide or the width of the fabric, then cut from it 7 bias strips 2¾" wide.

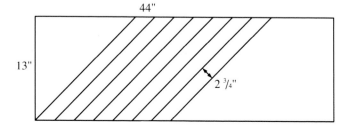

5. Cut 2 squares 10½" x 10½".

Basket Fabrics (cut the following from each fabric)
1. Cut 1 bias strip, 2¾" wide and about 13" long.
2. Cut 1 square 6⅞" x 6⅞", then cut it in half diagonally. OR, cut 1 of Template B.
3. Cut 1 square 2⅞" x 2⅞", then cut it in half diagonally. OR, cut 2 of Template A.

Floral Print
1. Cut 2 squares 17" x 17", then cut them in half diagonally twice to make 8 triangles. (You will need only 6 triangles.)

2. Cut 2 squares 10" x 10", then cut them in half diagonally to make 4 triangles.

Border
Cut 4 strips 3½" x 44" (or the width of the border fabric).

Piecing Instructions

Baskets
1. Prepare a strip unit by alternating the 7 bias background strips with the 6 basket fabric strips, beginning and ending with a background strip as shown. Press the seams open.

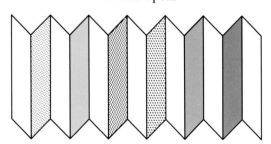

2. Following the instructions in the Lesson Box on speed piecing triangles, cut 7 squares 2½" x 2½" from each fabric combination.

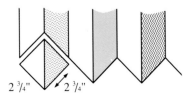

May Baskets *(May) by Joan Hanson, 1989, Seattle, Washington, 36″ x 50″. The lovely floral print is the "idea fabric" for these quick-to-piece baskets. Beautifully quilted by Hazel Montague.*

3. Assemble your Basket blocks as shown in the piecing diagram. Press seams toward the baskets.

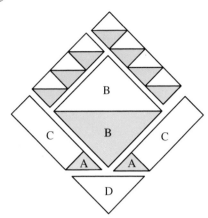

Assembling the Quilt

1. Assemble blocks and side triangles into diagonal rows as shown. Trim corners of triangles after stitching.

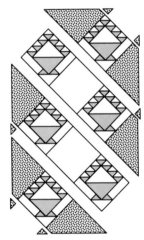

2. Add corner triangles.
3. Trim the edges so that the Basket blocks are 1" from the edge.

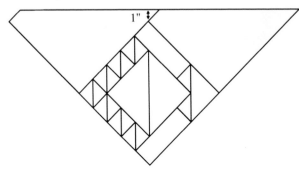

4. Sew the side borders on and then the top and bottom borders. For detailed instructions, see Adding Borders, page 93.

Quilting Suggestions

   This quilt really benefits from some fine hand quilting. The two plain squares will show off a lovely quilting design—with only 2 to do, why not go for it! Quilt a flower in each basket; use the design provided, or make up your own designs, or ask your children to draw some flowers for you. Outline quilt each basket. Quilt the floral chintz in a clamshell design. Quilt the border in a floral design that harmonizes with the design used in your plain blocks.

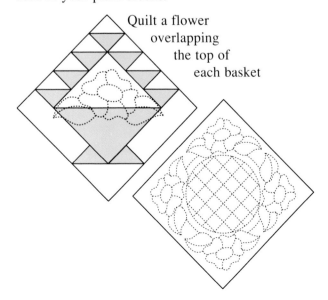

Quilt a flower overlapping the top of each basket

Lesson Boxes—May

Speed Piecing Triangles with the Bias Square®

A half-square triangle, as shown in the illustration, has the bias of the fabric along the long side and the straight of grain along the short sides. Two of these triangles make up a bias-square unit.

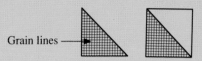

Grain lines

A quantity of bias-square units made up of 2 half-square triangles can be quickly pieced and cut when you use a Bias Square®.

Prepare a strip unit made up of bias strips. Cut each bias strip ¾" wider than the finished bias-square unit. In this Basket design, the finished size of the square is 2", so the bias strips are each cut 2¾" wide. Seam together, and press the seams open.

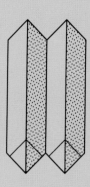

Use the Bias Square to cut squares as shown. In our Basket pattern, the size of the half-square triangle squares is 2½" x 2½" (2" finished), so we cut 2½" squares.

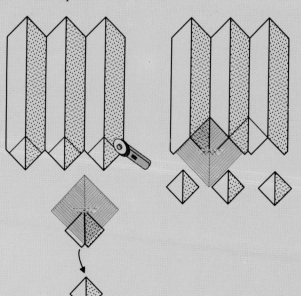

It may help to mark your cutting line on the underside of your Bias Square with tape, so you can more easily locate the size square you are cutting.

Diagonal Sets

Diagonally set quilts are made with blocks that are turned "on point" so that the straight of grain in each block runs diagonally. When this type of quilt is hung, it has a tendency to sag. To help control this tendency, cut the fill-in triangles that surround the blocks so that the straight of grain runs up and down. These triangles give support to the blocks and help stabilize them. However, when joining the blocks to the fill-in triangles, you will be joining a bias edge to a straight-of-grain edge, which can be tricky. If the bias cut edge is quite stretchy, you may want to stay-stitch in the seam allowance to keep it in shape.

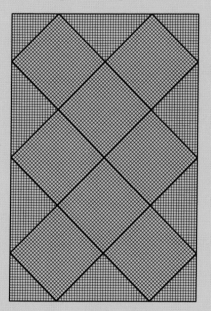

When the blocks and fill-in triangles are all joined, adding the outer border to the straight-of-grain edges of the fill-in triangles will further stabilize the quilt.

Space flower evenly for border design

One-quarter for a 10" block. Use 10" square of tracing paper to trace onto each quadrant, connecting lines.

Clamshell quilting design for floral triangles

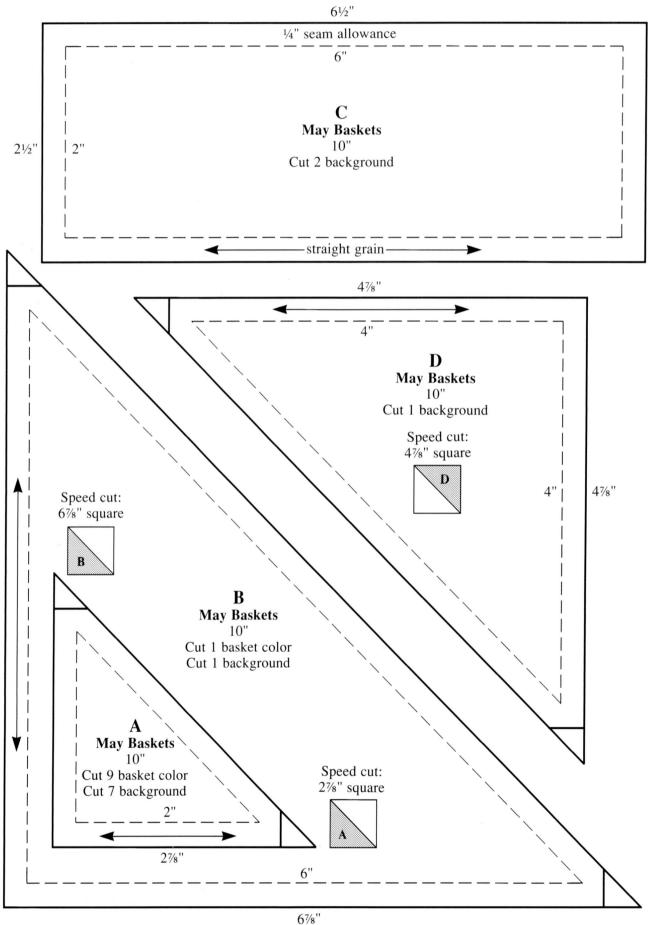

6½"

¼" seam allowance

6"

C
May Baskets
10"
Cut 2 background

2½"   2"

straight grain

4⅞"

4"

D
May Baskets
10"
Cut 1 background

Speed cut:
4⅞" square

D

4"   4⅞"

Speed cut:
6⅞" square

B

B
May Baskets
10"
Cut 1 basket color
Cut 1 background

A
May Baskets
10"
Cut 9 basket color
Cut 7 background

2"

Speed cut:
2⅞" square

A

2⅞"

2⅞"

6"

6⅞"

June: Grandpa's Ties

Lessons
Recycling Fabrics
Set-in Corners

This quilt is fun to make with recycled ties from someone special, in honor of Father's Day.

Quilt size: 36" x 40½"
Block size: 8½" x 10" (finished)
Number of blocks: 5 Bow Tie blocks and 4 necktie blocks

Fabric Required for Quilt Top
Old ties or fabric scraps for ties
1 yd. total of 1 to 5 colors for shirts
¼ yd. white for collars
¾ yd. solid OR 1½ yds. striped fabric for sashing and borders
18 shirt buttons (optional)

Cutting Instructions

Ties
If you are using old ties, see the Lesson Box on fabric recycling for hints on how to prepare them. Cut a bow tie or necktie from each old tie or from fabric scraps. Use Templates A and B for the 5 bow ties, and Templates H and L for the 4 neckties.

Shirts
Cut out the shirt pieces for each tie. Use Templates C, D, E, and F for the 5 bow ties, and Templates I, K, M, and N for the 4 neckties.

White Collars
Cut out collar pieces for each tie. Use Template G for the 5 bow ties, and Template J for the 4 neckties.

Border and Sashing
If you use a striped fabric for the borders and sashing strips, cut all pieces so that the stripes run vertically.
Vertical sashes: 2 strips 35" x 2½"
Horizontal sashes: 6 strips 9" x 2½"
Vertical side borders: 2 strips 41" x 3¾"
Horizontal top and bottom borders: 2 strips 30"x 3¾"

Piecing Instructions
1. Both blocks include set-in corners, where 2 patches form an angle and a third patch must be added into the angle. (See Set-in Corners in the Lesson Boxes for instructions.)

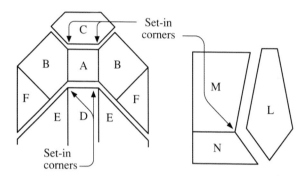

2. Refer to piecing diagrams and piece 5 bow tie and 4 necktie blocks.

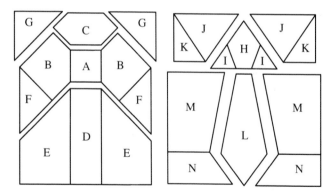

Assembling the Quilt
1. Arrange the blocks as shown. Sew the short sashing strips between the blocks to make 3 vertical rows.

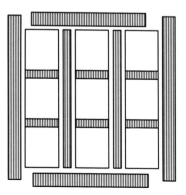

Grandpa's Ties *(June) by Joan Hanson, 1989, Seattle, Washington, 36" x 40½". My dear grandfather, who always came to Sunday dinner wearing a tie, inspired this quilt.*

Lesson Boxes—June

Recycling Fabrics

Unstitch old ties and discard the linings and interfacings. Hand wash them and dry them on a flat surface, pulling the grain lines back to shape because they were stretched on the bias when the tie was made. Spray starch or Fray-Check™ may help to stabilize the fabrics.

Set-in Corners

Perfect set-in corners can be achieved if you carefully mark and pin your pieces.

To sew the intersection correctly, all seams must meet ¼" from the edge. Make a dot to mark this point on each corner, using the templates as guides. If you have a ⅛" hole punch, punch a hole in the templates at these corners, and mark the fabric through the holes.

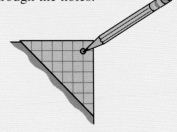

Match up the dots and edges on A and B. Stitch the seam to the dot and backstitch.

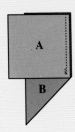

Add C, matching the dots. When you stitch, put the third piece on the underside so that the previous stitching line can be used as a guide.

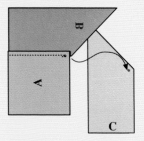

Stitch to the dot and backstitch.

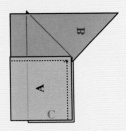

Stitch the other seam to the dot and backstitch. Press.

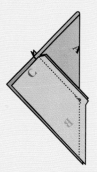

2. Sew on the 2 vertical sashing strips. Trim the ends off even.

3. Sew the side borders on, and then the top and bottom borders. For more detailed instructions, see Adding Borders, page 93.

4. Optional: Referring to the picture of the quilt, add shirt buttons, if desired.

Quilting Suggestions

Outline the ties and collars. Top-stitch on the collars and plackets. Quilt in shirt pockets, stripes, and the like.

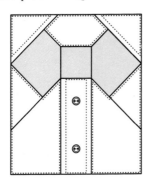
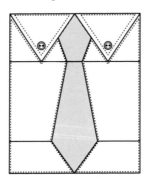

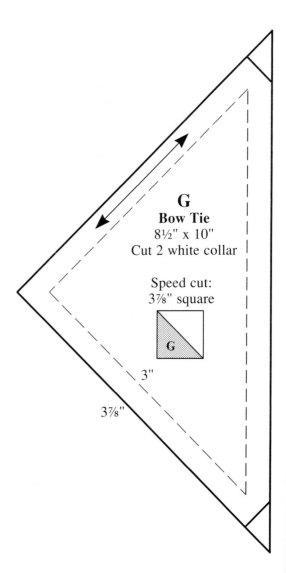

G
Bow Tie
8½" x 10"
Cut 2 white collar

Speed cut:
3⅞" square

3"

3⅞"

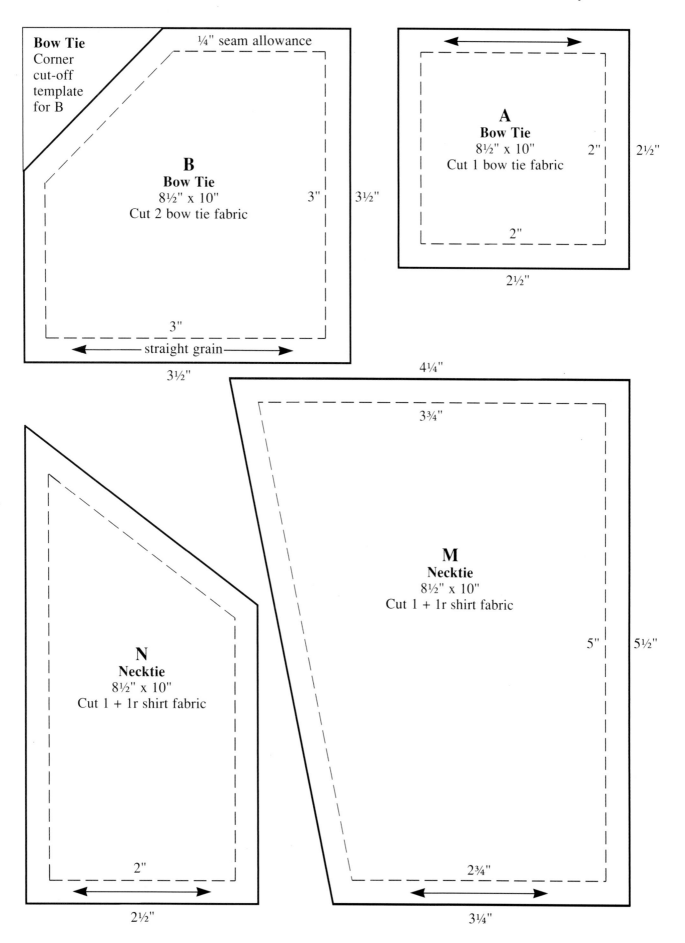

Bow Tie
Corner
cut-off
template
for B

¼" seam allowance

B
Bow Tie
8½" x 10"
Cut 2 bow tie fabric

3"

3"

3½"

3"

straight grain

3½"

A
Bow Tie
8½" x 10"
Cut 1 bow tie fabric

2"

2"

2"

2½"

2½"

2½"

4¼"

3¾"

M
Necktie
8½" x 10"
Cut 1 + 1r shirt fabric

5"

5½"

2¾"

3¼"

N
Necktie
8½" x 10"
Cut 1 + 1r shirt fabric

2"

2½"

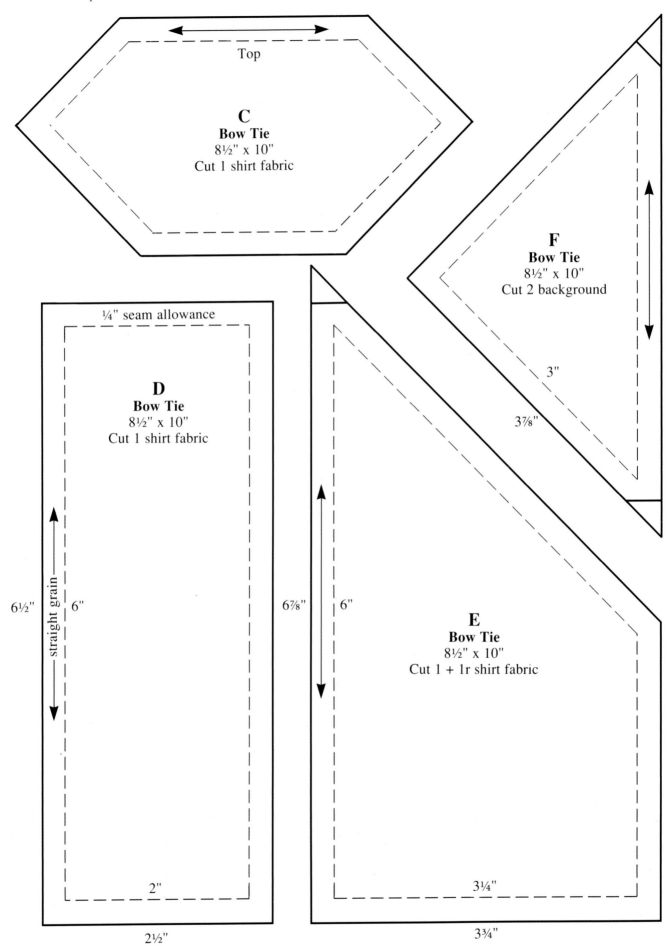

C
Bow Tie
8½" x 10"
Cut 1 shirt fabric

Top

F
Bow Tie
8½" x 10"
Cut 2 background

3"

3⅞"

¼" seam allowance

D
Bow Tie
8½" x 10"
Cut 1 shirt fabric

straight grain

6½"   6"

2"

2½"

6⅞"   6"

E
Bow Tie
8½" x 10"
Cut 1 + 1r shirt fabric

3¼"

3¾"

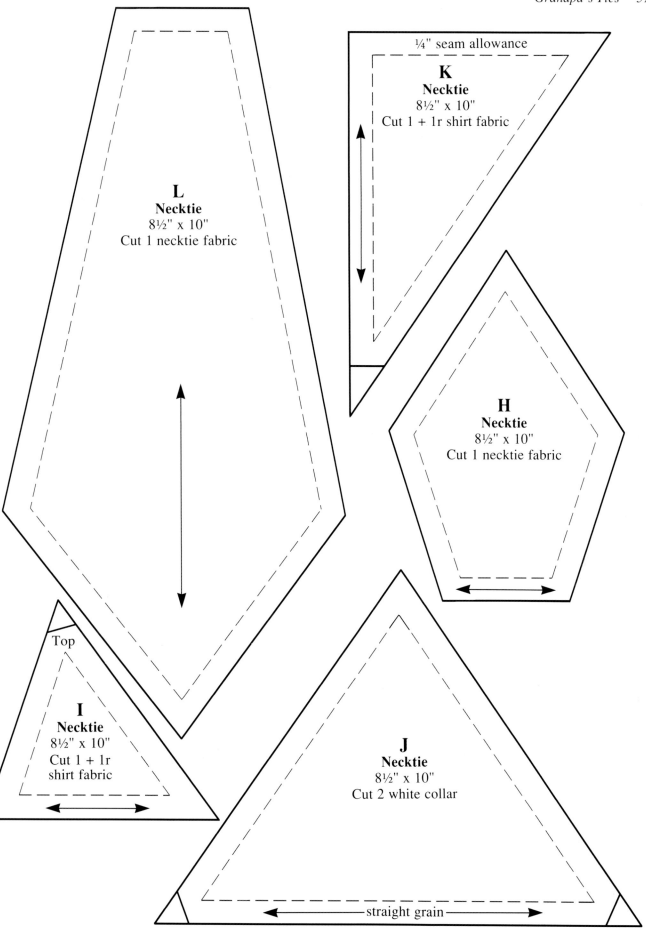

L
Necktie
8½" x 10"
Cut 1 necktie fabric

¼" seam allowance

K
Necktie
8½" x 10"
Cut 1 + 1r shirt fabric

H
Necktie
8½" x 10"
Cut 1 necktie fabric

Top

I
Necktie
8½" x 10"
Cut 1 + 1r
shirt fabric

J
Necktie
8½" x 10"
Cut 2 white collar

straight grain

July: Stars and Stripes

Lesson
Piecing 60° Angles

The asymmetrical setting of this quilt gives the effect of fireworks going off on a dark summer night. Sixty-degree triangles are easy to piece, and even though it may not look like it, there are no set-in corners in this design.

Quilt size: 36" x 46"

Fabric Required for Quilt Top
1 yd. blue solid for background
¼ yd. each of 5 blue prints for stars
¼ yd. each of 5 tan prints for star stripes and centers
¼ yd. each of 5 red prints for star stripes and centers
½ yd. border fabric

Cutting Instructions

Background Blue (solid)
1. Cut 2 of Template A.
2. Cut 7 of Template B (if you use a fabric with right and wrong sides, such as a print, cut 4 of Template B and 3 of Template B reversed).
3. Cut 4 of Template C (if you use a fabric with right and wrong sides, cut 2 of Template C and 2 of Template C reversed).
4. Cut 1 of Template D.
5. Cut 3 of Template E (if you use a fabric with right and wrong sides, cut 2 of Template E and 2 of Template E reversed).
6. Cut 1 of Template F.

Blue Prints
Cut 6 of Template A from each of the 5 blue prints.

Tan Prints
1. Make 2 cuts of each of the 5 tan prints, 1⅜" wide.
2. Cut 3 of Template A from each of the 5 tan prints.

Red Prints
1. Make 2 cuts of each of the 5 red prints, 1⅜" wide.
2. Cut 3 of Template A from each of the 5 red prints.

Border
Make 4 cuts, each 3" wide.

Piecing Instructions
1. Make 5 strip units using the 2 red print strips and the 2 tan print strips from each fabric, alternating colors as shown and arranging the fabrics to your liking. Press all seam allowances toward the red prints.

Red
Tan
Red
Tan

2. Using Template A, cut 12 triangles. Repeat for all 5 strip units.

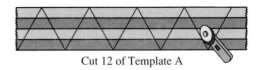

Cut 12 of Template A

3. Six of the triangles will have a red bottom, and six will have a tan bottom.
4. Arrange all pieces according to the illustration of the quilt below. This is like putting a puzzle together.

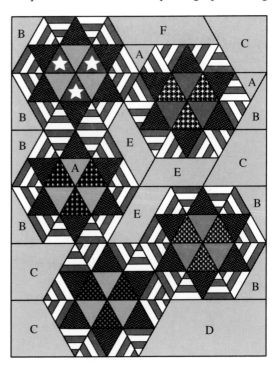

Stars and Stripes *(July) by Joan Hanson, 1989, Seattle, Washington, 36" x 46". This quilt reminds me of fireworks exploding in a dark summer sky.*

5. To avoid set-in corners, start at the top of the quilt and assemble the pieces in sections as shown. Pick up 2 or 3 pieces at a time, sew them together, and return them to the layout. It's easy to get confused, so don't pick up too many at one time!

6. Press the seam allowances in each row before you sew it to another row; each seam allowance should be pressed before it is crossed by another seam.

7. When the pieces are all assembled, sew the side borders on, and then the top and bottom borders. For more detailed instructions, see Adding Borders, page 93.

Quilting Suggestions

Use the star designs on the next page and quilt stars at random in the blue background areas. The small stars could be quilted in the border, connected with lines as illustrated.

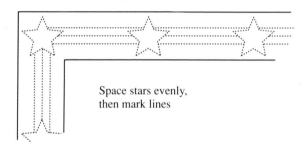

Space stars evenly, then mark lines

Or, quilt in overall wavy lines, quilting stars at random as shown in the photograph on page 53.

Lesson Box—July

Piecing 60° Angles

Using 60° triangles is a good way to achieve movement in a quilt; it creates diagonal lines that are quite simple to piece. At first glance, the piecing looks complicated, since we are accustomed to looking for the square unit block in a quilt. To piece with 60° angles, first work out your design on a 60° angle grid. (You can purchase 60° triangle graph paper.) Then any areas that form the background or larger shapes can be drafted out at actual size. Be sure to add ¼" seam allowances.

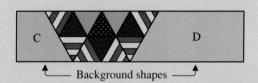

Background shapes

Work on a flannel board to place all pieces where they belong. When you are ready to piece your quilt together, disregard the design and piece by rows. Pick up 2 or 3 pieces at a time to make larger units, until you finally have rows sewn. Be sure to press each seam before it is crossed by another.

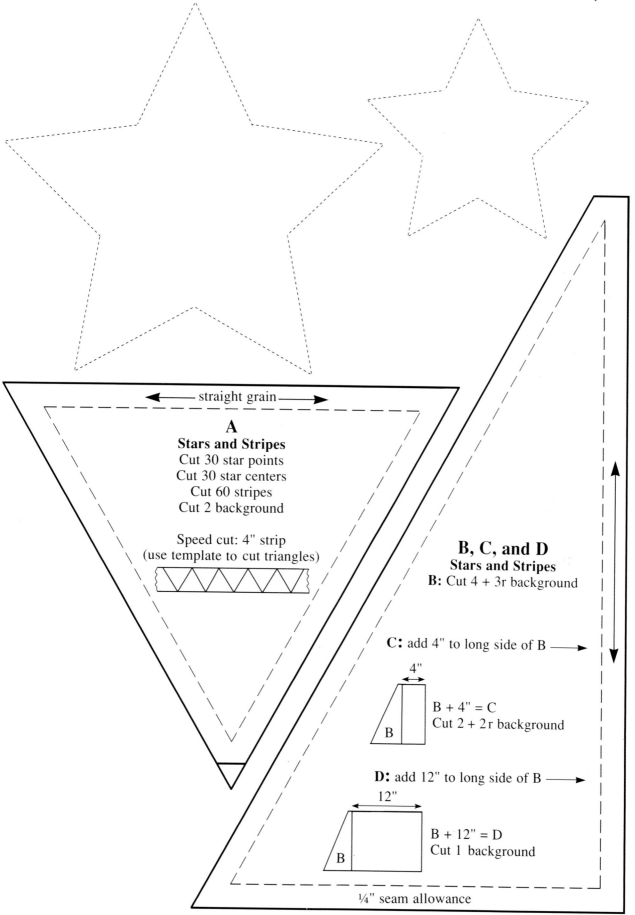

straight grain

A
Stars and Stripes
Cut 30 star points
Cut 30 star centers
Cut 60 stripes
Cut 2 background

Speed cut: 4" strip
(use template to cut triangles)

B, C, and D
Stars and Stripes
B: Cut 4 + 3r background

C: add 4" to long side of B ⟶

4"

B + 4" = C
Cut 2 + 2r background

B

D: add 12" to long side of B ⟶

12"

B + 12" = D
Cut 1 background

B

¼" seam allowance

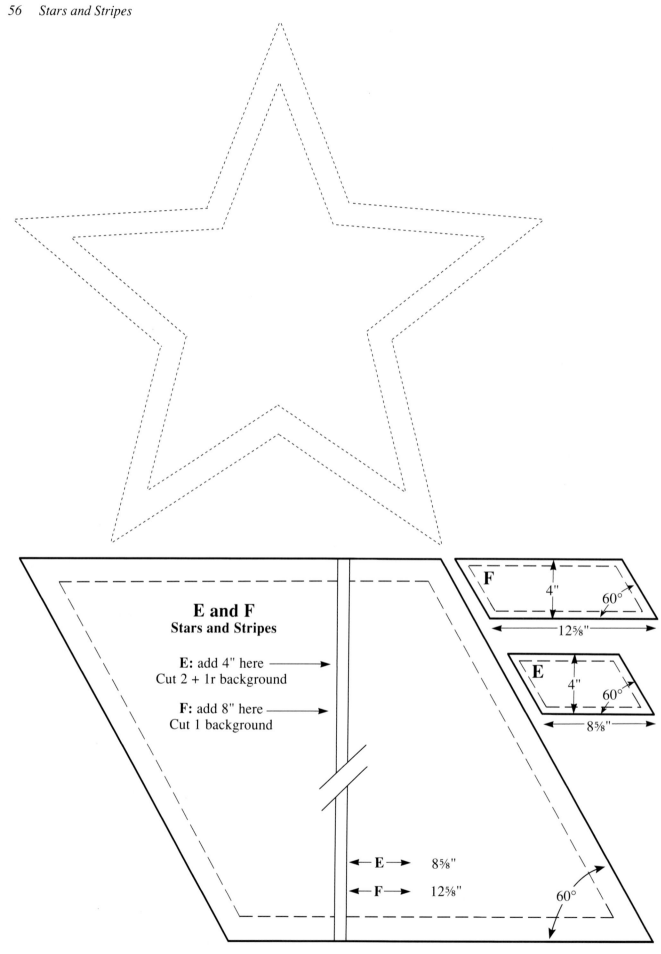

E and F
Stars and Stripes

E: add 4" here ⟶
Cut 2 + 1r background

F: add 8" here ⟶
Cut 1 background

⟵ **E** ⟶   8⅝"
⟵ **F** ⟶   12⅝"

60°

F
4"   60°
12⅝"

E
4"   60°
8⅝"

August: Beach Balls

Lessons
Curved Seams, by Hand or Machine
Strip-Pieced Borders

This quilt reminds me of beach balls and beach umbrellas on a sunny day. If you are looking for a small summer take-along project, this quilt with hand-pieced curves may be just the answer.

Quilt size: 36" x 48"
Block size: 6" (finished)
Number of blocks: 24 beach ball blocks

Fabric Required for Quilt Top

⅛ yd. each of 30 prints, all colors (or 44"-wide scraps)
¼ yd. each of 6 solids, all colors
½ yd. inner border solid and ½ yd. outer border solid (or 1 yd. total of 1 border solid)

Cutting Instructions

Prints

Make 1 cut 1¹¹⁄₁₆" wide of each of 30 print fabrics. You will need to cut between the 1⅝" and 1¾" marks on your acrylic ruler. Put a piece of masking tape on the ruler to help you find the place for each cut.

Solids

From each of 6 colors, cut 8 quarter-circles using Template B. OR, cut 2 circles 7" in diameter and use Template B to cut them into quarters.

Borders

For inner border, cut 4 strips 2" x 44". For outer border, cut 4 strips 3½" x 44".

Piecing Instructions

Multicolor Strips

1. Divide the print cuts into 6 groups of 5 cuts each. You may want to group them randomly, or group them by color or by lights and darks. Make 6 strip units from the strips. Press all seam allowances in the same direction. The strip units should measure 6½" wide. Check the first one and adjust your seam allowance if you are off.

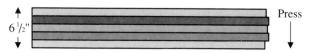

2. From each strip unit, cut 4 squares 6½" x 6½".

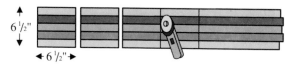

3. Using Template A, cut a quarter-circle off 2 opposite corners of each square.

Be sure to work with the right side of the block facing up and line up the arrows on the template with the strip seams, or your blocks will be backward.

Curved Seams

1. Two solid quarter-circles are sewn to each striped piece to make the block.

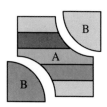

2. See the Lesson Boxes for instructions on sewing curved seams. Sew on all the cut-out curves. Press the seams toward the quarter-circles.

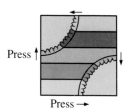

Beach Balls *(August) by Joan Hanson, 1989, Seattle, Washington, 36" x 48". For this quilt, I chose fabrics that reminded me of 1930s fabrics. The result is quite colorful!*

Assembling the Quilt

1. Lay out the blocks as shown in the illustration of the quilt, and rearrange them until you are happy with the distribution of colors. Sew the blocks together in rows, then sew the rows to each other.

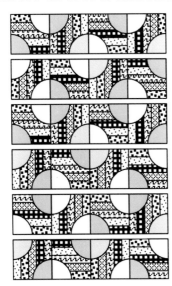

2. Add the inner border strips to the sides, then the top and bottom. Repeat with the outer border strips. For more detailed instructions, see Adding Borders, page 93.

Optional Pieced Border

1. Using the leftover sets of strips, cut 4 pieces 3" wide from each strip.

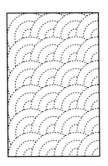 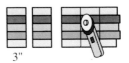

3"

2. Sew these together in sections long enough for the side, top, and bottom borders. Be sure to mix up the colors.
3. For instructions on how to add this type of border to your quilt, see Strip-Pieced Borders in the Lesson Boxes.
4. Last, add the outer solid border.

Quilting Suggestions

This quilt might be quilted in overall fans, or overall diagonal lines.

Or, outline quilt each beach ball and quilt a diagonal line through the blocks.

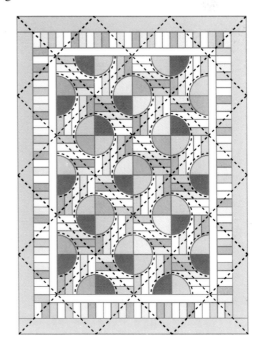

Lesson Boxes—August

Curved Seams, by Hand or Machine

Curved seams may be sewn by hand or on the sewing machine. The technique is basically the same using either method.

Locate the center of each curved seam by folding the fabric in half. Pin the solid quarter-circle and the striped piece together at the centers. Pin through the seam allowances at each end.

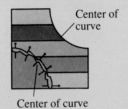

Center of curve

Center of curve

Gently stretch the inner curve (the striped piece) to fit it to the outer curve (the solid piece). You can make a few clips into the inner-curve seam allowance.

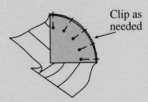

Clip as needed

Start stitching by hand or machine at the center pin and sew out to the end. Start again at the center and sew out to the other end.

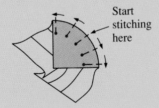

Start stitching here

If you are sewing by hand, do not knot your thread but leave a 6" tail when you stitch from the center to the other end. Rethread this tail to complete the seam to the other end.

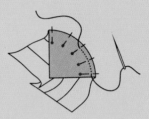

Strip-Pieced Borders

A simple but striking pieced border can be made from strips of fabric sewn together into a strip unit. Make crosscuts the width you want your border.

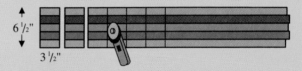

6½"

3½"

Sew the crosscuts together to make strips to fit the 4 sides of your quilt. The top and bottom strips are the width of your quilt to this point, plus one width of your border; the sides are the length of your quilt to this point, plus one width of your border, as follows: quilt width, 27", plus width of border, 2½", equals length of top and bottom, or 29½". Quilt length, 36", plus width of border, 2½", equals length of sides, or 38½".

Starting in the upper left corner, sew on the pieced border strip. Stop stitching 2" before you reach the end.

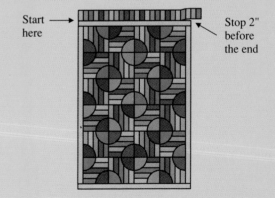

Start here

Stop 2" before the end

Now add the left-side pieced border.

Next add the bottom pieced border, then the right side.

Now go back and finish the seam attaching the top pieced border.

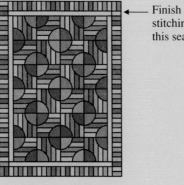

← Finish
stitching
this seam

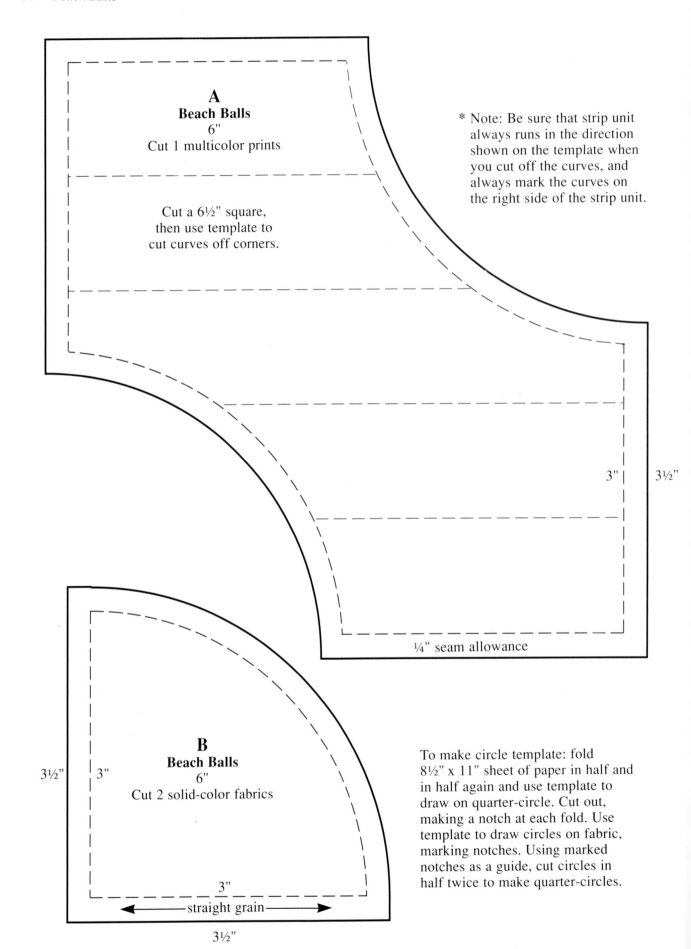

A
Beach Balls
6"
Cut 1 multicolor prints

Cut a 6½" square,
then use template to
cut curves off corners.

* Note: Be sure that strip unit
always runs in the direction
shown on the template when
you cut off the curves, and
always mark the curves on
the right side of the strip unit.

3"

3½"

¼" seam allowance

B
Beach Balls
6"
Cut 2 solid-color fabrics

3½"   3"

3"

straight grain

3½"

To make circle template: fold
8½" x 11" sheet of paper in half and
in half again and use template to
draw on quarter-circle. Cut out,
making a notch at each fold. Use
template to draw circles on fabric,
marking notches. Using marked
notches as a guide, cut circles in
half twice to make quarter-circles.

September: School Daze

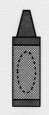

Lesson
Precision Piecing

What fun it would be to use leftover fabrics from a child's school clothes to dress these four happy students and then personalize their hair and eye colors. To make a thank-you gift for a special teacher, have students sign their names in the outer border.

Quilt size: 36" x 49"
Block size: 6½" x 7" (finished)

Fabric Required for Quilt Top

¼ yd. each of 6 colors for crayon wrappers
⅛ yd. each of 6 colors for crayon ends and points
¼ yd. for schoolhouse roof (or scrap)
¼ yd. for schoolhouse side and door (or scrap)
⅛ yd. for schoolhouse window (or scrap)
⅛ yd. for schoolhouse front and belfry (or scrap)
¼ yd. for schoolhouse roof point (or scrap)
⅛ yd. for school kids' faces and hands, and girls' legs
⅛ yd. each of 8–10 colors for school kids' clothes and
   shoes (or scraps)
¾ yd. background
½ yd. sashing
½ yd. border

Cutting Instructions

Crayons

1. Cut 1 piece 4½" x 13" from each of the 6 wrapper fabrics (each will later be cut into 5 crayons).
2. Cut 2 pieces 1" x 13" of each crayon color for the ends; cut 5 of each color from Template A for the points.

School Kids

1. Cut 4 from Template P for faces.
2. Cut 8 from Template T for hands.
3. For girls:
   a. Cut 2 from Template S (1¼" x 6") for sleeves (1 from each dress fabric).
   b. Cut 2 from Template U for 2 dresses (1 from each dress fabric).
   c. Cut 4 from Template X for girls' legs.
   d. Cut 4 from Template W (1¼" x 1") for girls' shoes.

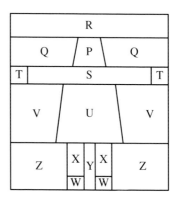

4. For boys:
   a. Cut 2 from Template S (1¼" x 6") for shirts (1 from each shirt fabric).
   b. Cut 2 from Template C1 for shirts (1 from each shirt fabric).
   c. Cut 2 plus 2 reversed from Template B1 for pants (1 of each from each pants fabric).
   d. Cut 4 from Template W (1¼" x 1") for boys' shoes.

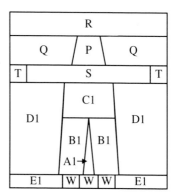

Background

1. For schoolhouse, cut:
   2 from Template J
   1 from Template K plus 1 from Template K reversed
   1 from Template M* (5½" x 13½")
   1 from Template N (4½" x 5½")
   1 from Template O* (4½" x 15½")
   * No template given

2. For crayons, cut 30 from Template A.
3. For kids, cut:
    4 from Template R (1½" x 7½")
    4 from Template Q plus 4 from Template Q reversed
    2 from Template V plus 2 from Template V reversed
    2 from Template Y (1" x 2½")
    4 from Template Z (2½" x 3")
    2 from Template A1
    2 from Template D1 plus 2 from Template D1 reversed
    2 from Template W (1¼" x 1")
    4 from Template E1 (1" x 3")

Schoolhouse

Cut pieces from your schoolhouse fabrics as shown in the diagram, using Templates B, C, D, E, F, H, I, J, K, and L. Measurements are shown for the larger squares and rectangles, which you will need to rotary cut.

Sashing

Make eight 2" cuts the width of the fabric (5 for the horizontal sashing and 3 to piece the vertical sashing).

Border

Make 4 cuts, each 3½" wide.

Piecing Instructions

Crayons

1. Stitch a 1" x 13" crayon end to each side of a 4½" x 13" wrapper. Press the seams toward the wrapper. Crosscut into 5 crayons, each 2½" wide.

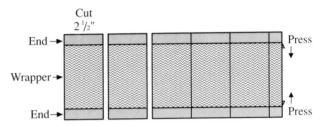

2. Arrange crayons into 2 rows of 14 crayons each. (You will have 2 left over.) Sew the crayons to each other and press the seams open.

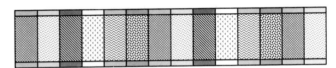

3. Measure the rows of crayons. Is each 28½" long? If not, make adjustments.

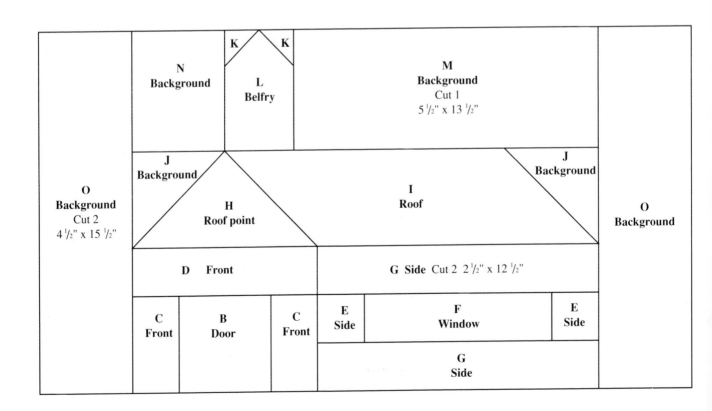

School Daze *(September) by Joan Hanson, 1989, Seattle, Washington, 36" x 49". These happy children are on their way to the first day of school. The ruler in the border was drawn by hand with a broad-point fabric marking pen.*

Lesson Box—September

Precision Piecing

The tricky part to piecing this quilt is in getting each row to measure 28½", since each row has a different number of vertical seams. If the schoolhouse is too wide, the background at the sides can be trimmed, but the crayons and kids must be adjusted between each block. This is a challenge to your accuracy. Let's hope you get it right (or close) the first try!

It's important to measure each row as you go along, so you are consistently measuring the same width as other rows. If you are off just a little, aggressive pressing with a good steam iron sometimes will do the trick. This can stretch things out just a bit or push everything together just a bit, as cotton fabric does have some give.

If that doesn't do the trick, check your templates to make sure your pieces were cut accurately. Also check your seam allowances.

If your pieced strips are too wide, restitch just inside every other seam. When there are a lot of seams, this can shorten the strip a surprising amount. If the pieced strips are too short, rip out several of the seams one by one and restitch just outside your old sewing line. Keep checking the length of the strip as you go, and stop when you arrive at the right size. Hopefully, adjoining seams will line up after all the adjusting. Good luck!

4. Lay the rows of crayons out, and above them arrange the crayon tips.

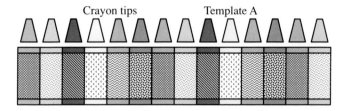

5. Stitch the 2 rows of crayon tips together, with a background piece between each one, beginning and ending the row with a background piece.

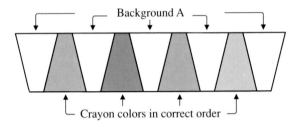

6. Line up the rows of points on top of each crayon row and stitch together. Does each tip line up with the crayon? Adjust the seams as needed so they line up and each row measures 28½". Trim the background pieces at each end.

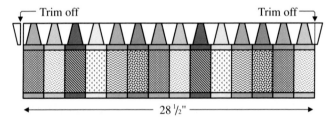

School Kids

1. Lay out the pieces for the boys and girls next to your sewing machine, following the diagrams on page 63.
2. Note that some of the pieces are just slightly larger at the top than at the bottom, or vice versa (U, V, B1, C1, D1), and make sure that you have everything right side up. Use the templates as guides, as the top is marked on each. Stitch together in alphabetical order in rows. Measure each block: is each 7½" wide? If not, make adjustments. Stitch all 4 together: is the row 28½" wide?

Schoolhouse

1. Lay out the pieces next to your sewing machine, following the diagram on page 64.
2. Piece together in alphabetical order in 3 rows: house sides and front (B-G), roof (H-J), and belfry (K-N). Add side pieces. Does the section measure 28½" wide? If it is too wide, trim the O side pieces. If it is too small, let out the seams at O. If necessary, cut new, wider O's.

Sashing and Borders

1. Stitch the 5 sashing strips between the rows and on the top and bottom.

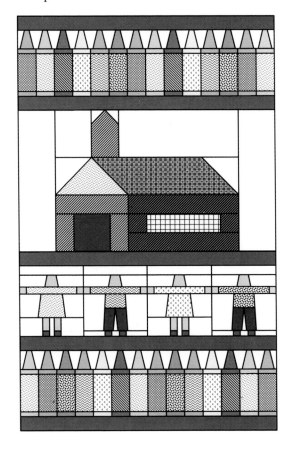

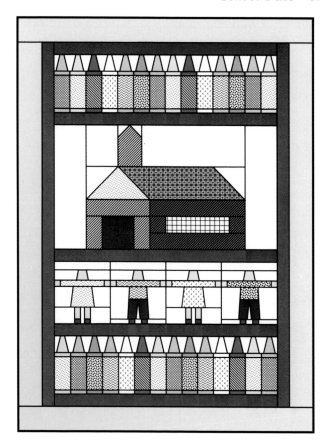

2. Next add the 2 vertical sashing strips to both sides. You may have to piece them to make strips long enough.
3. Finally, add the border strips to both sides, and then the top and bottom. If there are going to be signatures in this border, press freezer paper to the back of the fabric to stabilize it. Pilot SC-UF pens are permanent and come in a variety of colors. Be sure to test your pen on your fabric for colorfastness before using it for signatures.

Quilting and Finishing Suggestions

Quilt an oval in each crayon wrapper for the label.

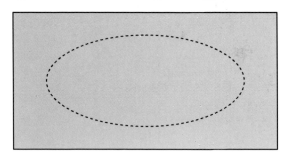

Outline quilt the crayons, school kids, and schoolhouse. Quilt in details such as window panes in the schoolhouse, doors, a bell in the belfry, the name of the school, and bricks on the walls. The background can be quilted in diagonal lines. Embellish the schoolhouse and kids with embroidery, buttons, seed beads, and the like.

Q
School Daze
Boy and Girl
7" x 7½"
Cut 1 + 1r

¼" seam allowance

P
School Daze
Boy and Girl

7" x 7½"
Cut 1 body fabric

R
School Daze
Boy and Girl
7" x 7½"
Cut 1
background

7"   7½"

1"

1½"

T
¾"
¾"

1¼"

1¼"

T
School Daze Boy and Girl
7" x 7½"
Cut 2 body fabric

S
School Daze Boy and Girl
7" x 7½"
Cut 1 dress (girl) or shirt (boy)

5½"   6"

¾"

1¼"

U
School Daze Girl
7" x 7½"
Cut 1 dress

straight grain

Top

V
School Daze Girl
7" x 7½"
Cut 1 + 1r background

Top

3"   2½"

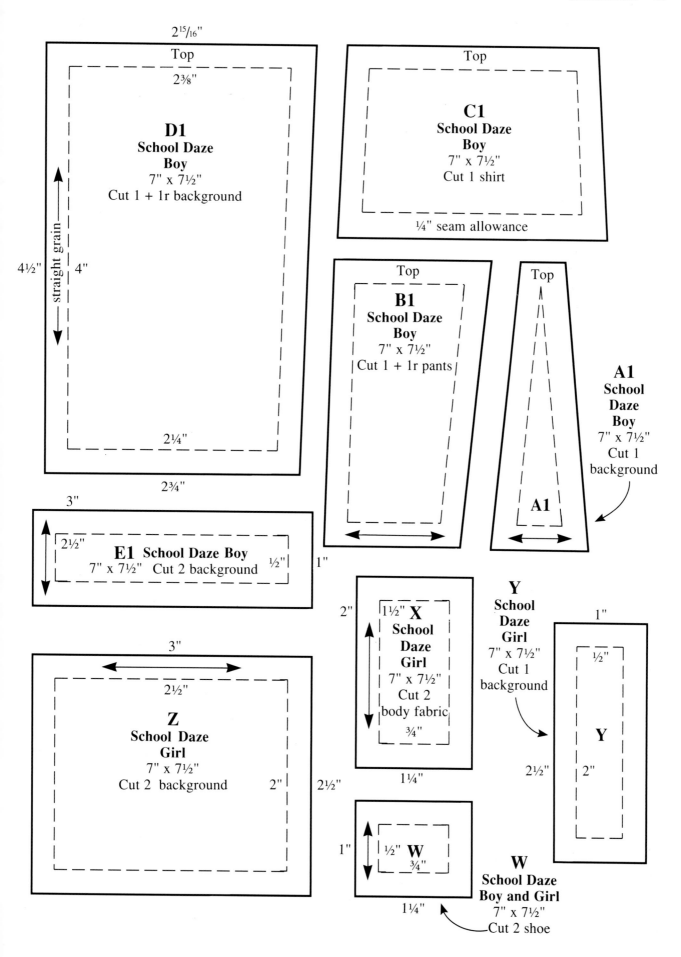

D1
School Daze
Boy
7" x 7½"
Cut 1 + 1r background

2¹⁵/₁₆"
Top
2⅜"
4½"
4"
straight grain
2¼"
2¾"

C1
School Daze
Boy
7" x 7½"
Cut 1 shirt

Top
¼" seam allowance

B1
School Daze
Boy
7" x 7½"
Cut 1 + 1r pants

Top

A1
School Daze
Boy
7" x 7½"
Cut 1
background

Top
A1

E1 **School Daze Boy**
7" x 7½" Cut 2 background

3"
2½"
½"
1"

X
School Daze
Girl
7" x 7½"
Cut 2
body fabric

2"
1½"
¾"
1¼"
2½"

Y
School Daze
Girl
7" x 7½"
Cut 1
background

1"
½"
Y
2"
2½"

Z
School Daze
Girl
7" x 7½"
Cut 2 background

3"
2½"
2"

W
½"
¾"
1"
1¼"

W
School Daze
Boy and Girl
7" x 7½"
Cut 2 shoe

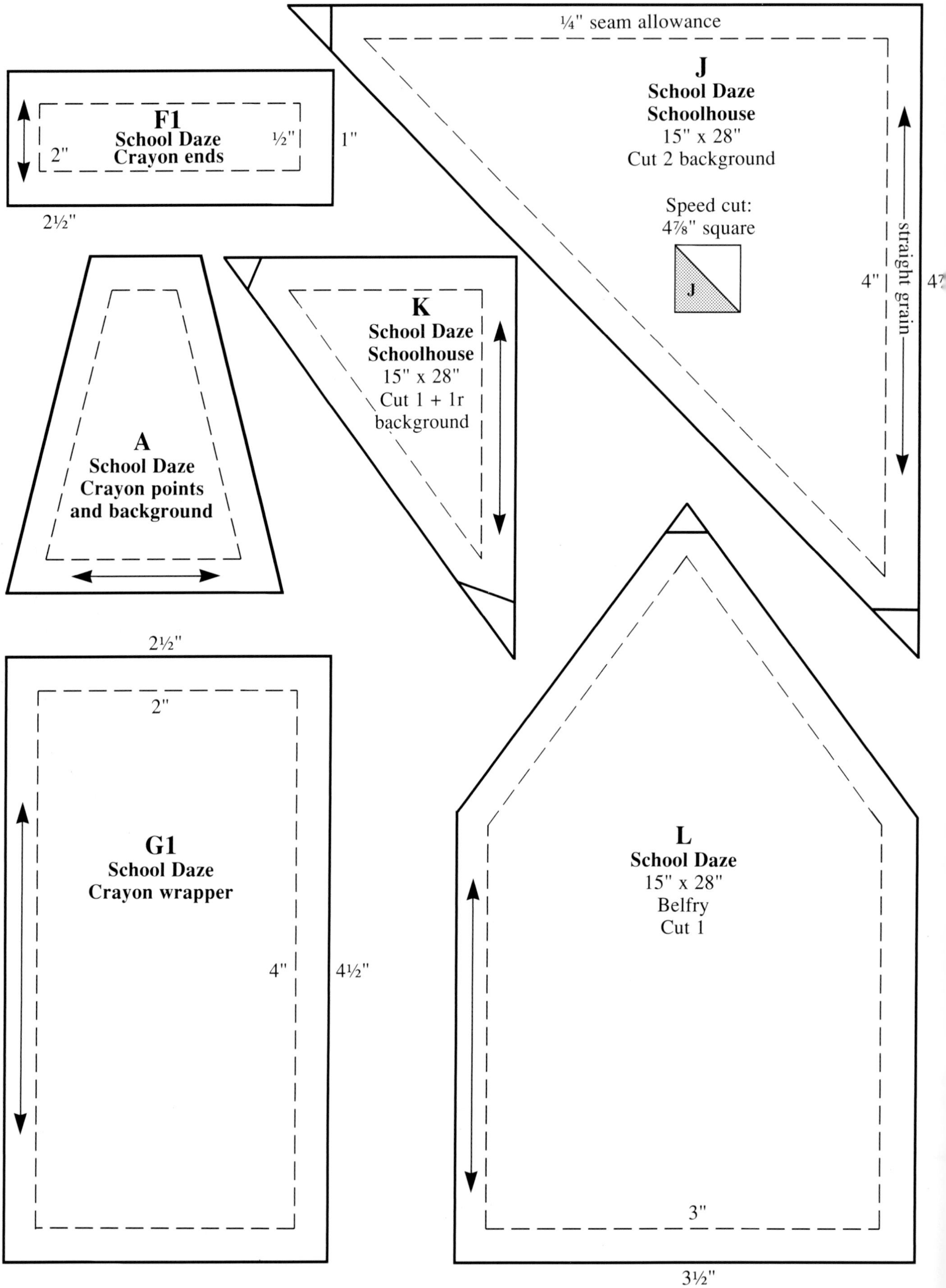

F1
School Daze
Crayon ends
½"
1"
2"
2½"

J
School Daze
Schoolhouse
15" x 28"
Cut 2 background

¼" seam allowance

Speed cut:
4⅞" square

J

4"

straight grain

A
School Daze
Crayon points
and background

K
School Daze
Schoolhouse
15" x 28"
Cut 1 + 1r
background

2½"
2"

G1
School Daze
Crayon wrapper

4"
4½"

L
School Daze
15" x 28"
Belfry
Cut 1

3"
3½"

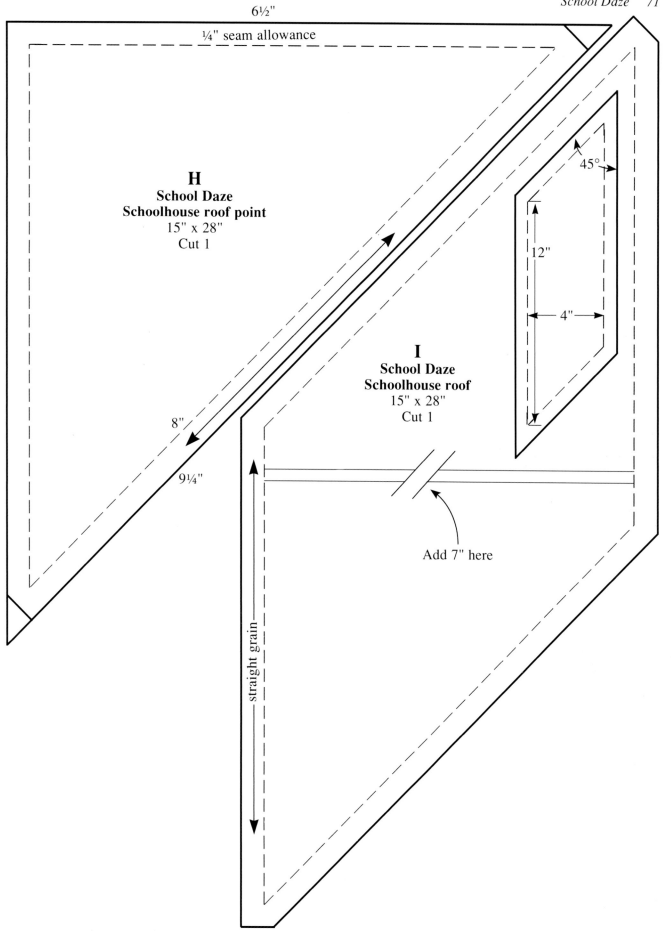

6½"

¼" seam allowance

H
School Daze
Schoolhouse roof point
15" x 28"
Cut 1

45°

12"

4"

I
School Daze
Schoolhouse roof
15" x 28"
Cut 1

8"

9¼"

Add 7" here

straight grain

6½"

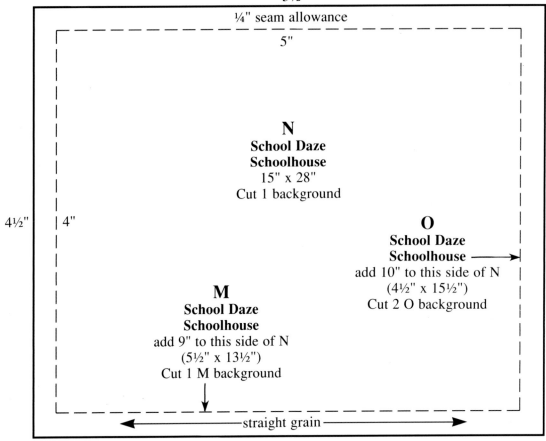

5½"

¼" seam allowance

5"

4½"   4"

N
School Daze
Schoolhouse
15" x 28"
Cut 1 background

O
School Daze
Schoolhouse ——⟶
add 10" to this side of N
(4½" x 15½")
Cut 2 O background

M
School Daze
Schoolhouse
add 9" to this side of N
(5½" x 13½")
Cut 1 M background

⟵———straight grain———⟶

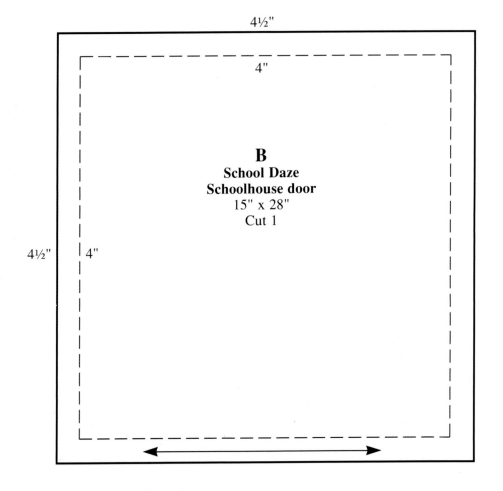

4½"

4"

4½"   4"

B
School Daze
Schoolhouse door
15" x 28"
Cut 1

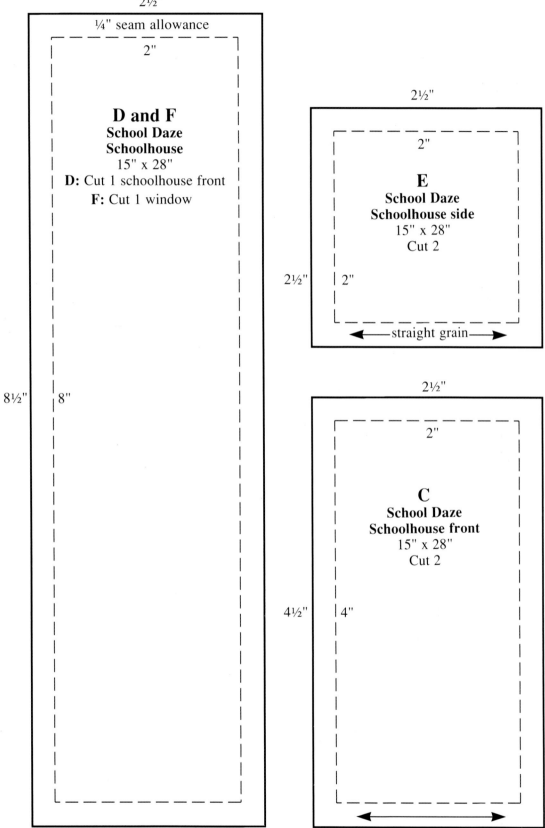

2½"

¼" seam allowance

2"

D and F
School Daze
Schoolhouse
15" x 28"
D: Cut 1 schoolhouse front
F: Cut 1 window

8½"   8"

2½"

2"

E
School Daze
Schoolhouse side
15" x 28"
Cut 2

2½"   2"

←—straight grain—→

2½"

2"

C
School Daze
Schoolhouse front
15" x 28"
Cut 2

4½"   4"

October: Falling Leaves

Lessons
Bias-Bar Appliqué
Speedy Triangles

The warm tones of fall make an interesting color study, and arranging the quilt's leaves and border squares is a lot of fun. The quilt can have a very controlled look if each leaf is made from the same print and set pointing up, or a very random look can be achieved by mixing up the triangle leaf points and reversing some of the leaves, setting them so they look like they are blowing into a pile on a crisp, windy fall day. See examples in the Gallery of Quilts, pages 9–14.

Quilt size: 36" x 46"
Block size: 6" x 8" (finished)
Number of blocks: 13 leaf blocks and 12 plain blocks

Fabric Required for Quilt Top
1¼ yds. background
¼ yd. each of 13 leaf colors
¼ yd. medium brown for stems
Also needed: a ¼" metal bias bar

Cutting Instructions

Background
1. Cut the inner border strips from the length of the background fabric, parallel to the selvage edges. There is less stretch in this direction than if the strips were cut crosswise, making it easier to achieve a nice flat edge around the quilt. For the inner border, cut 2 strips 1½" x 41", and 2 strips 1½" x 34".
2. From the rest of the background fabric, cut:
   12 rectangles 6½" x 8½" for plain blocks
   26 squares 2½" x 2½" (Template A)

13 rectangles 2½" x 6½" (Template D)
13 rectangles for speedy triangles, 3½" x 6½" (Template E)

Leaf Fabric (cut the following from each fabric)
1. Cut 7 squares 2½" x 2½" (Template A); one is for the leaf block and 6 are for the border.
2. Cut 1 rectangle 2½" x 4½" (Template B).
3. Cut 1 rectangle for speedy triangles, 3½" x 6½" (Template E).

Stem Fabric
From the ¼ yard, cut 7 bias strips, each ¾" wide.

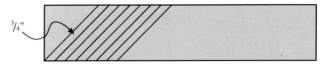

Piecing Instructions
1. See Bias-Bar Appliqué in the Lesson Boxes for instructions for the stems. Each of your bias strips is long enough to make two 6" stems; you will need 13 stems.
2. To speed-piece the leaf triangles to the background triangles, follow the instructions for Speedy Triangles in the Lesson Boxes, using 1 set for each leaf.
3. To assemble each leaf, follow the piecing diagram.

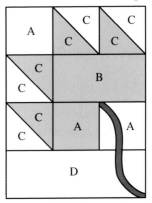

For the top row, sew 2 of the speedy-triangle squares together and add a square (Template A) of background fabric. Press the seams toward the background square.

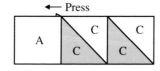

4. For the next row, sew leaf fabric rectangle (Template B) to another speedy-triangle square. Press the seam toward the rectangle.

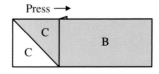

More Falling Leaves *(October) by Joan Hanson, 1990, Seattle, Washington, 36" x 46". The fabrics in this quilt are similar to those in Autumn Vintage (page 10). In contrast to that quilt, half the blocks were pieced in reverse here, the stems curve randomly, and the leaf points are all mixed up for a more windblown look. You decide which you like best.*

Lesson Boxes—October

Bias-Bar Appliqué

To prepare a bias appliqué stem, fold a ¾" bias strip in half lengthwise and stitch ¼" from the folded edge. This will leave a ⅛" seam allowance.

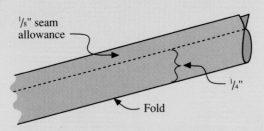

Insert a ¼" metal bias bar, roll the seam to the underside, and press.

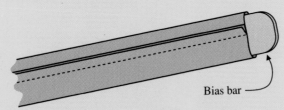

Remove the bias bar.

Speedy Triangles

The idea behind this method is that it is more accurate and efficient to stitch the bias seam joining 2 triangles before the bias edges are cut. The method works well for just a few half-square triangles or for many. The limitation with this method, as opposed to the method used in the May Baskets quilt, is that you use just 2 fabrics instead of using many fabrics for a scrappy look.

You can use this method for any size triangle. To determine how large a square to use for your grid, add ⅞" to the measurement of your finished half-square triangle square for seam allowance. For example, if you want 1" finished squares for a Feathered Star block, make your squares 1⅞". Or, if you want 4" finished squares, make your squares 4⅞". The ⅞" seam allowance always remains the same.

Once you have determined how large the squares are to be, determine how many finished squares you will need. Each square of the grid you will draw will make 2 finished squares, each made up of a light and a dark half-square triangle. Cut 1 piece of each of your fabrics large enough to accommodate the number of squares you need.

Mark squares on the wrong side of the lightest fabric in a grid pattern as shown. Use your see-through acrylic ruler. After you have marked the grid, draw diagonal lines through the squares

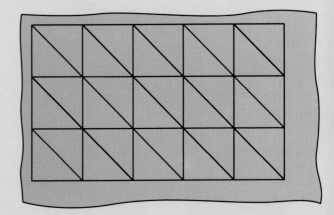

The lines you have marked are all cutting lines. If you want to mark stitching lines, mark ¼" on both sides of the diagonal lines.

To speed-piece 4 half-square triangles for each leaf block, cut a rectangle of leaf fabric and a rectangle of background fabric 3½" x 6½" (Template E). With a pencil, trace the solid lines of Template E on the wrong side of the background fabric. If you cannot see through your background fabric to trace the lines, photocopy Template E or trace it on a separate piece of paper, tape the copy on a lighted window, and then trace the lines onto your background fabric.

Place your 2 fabrics right sides together and with the marked side of the background fabric on top, stitch ¼" from the lines, following the arrows on Template E.

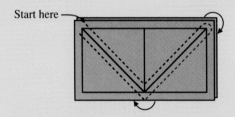

Cut apart on the solid lines. Open the pieces up; you now have 4 leaf triangles accurately pieced to 4 background triangles. Press the seams toward the darker fabric and trim off the little corner triangles.

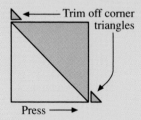

5. Partially assemble the third row: sew a square of leaf fabric (Template A) to a speedy-triangle square, then add a square of background fabric (Template A) but sew only the bottom half of the seam. Press the seams toward the speedy triangle.

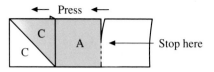

6. Sew the third row to background rectangle (Template D). Press the seam toward the background rectangle.

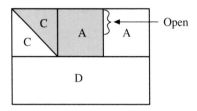

7. Machine baste the stem onto the third and fourth rows, so that the stem forms a gentle curve to your liking. The stems can all look the same, or each one can be different. Extend the bottom raw edge of the stem past the bottom corner of the block, and extend the top raw edge of the stem past the corner of the background square (Template A) in the third row.

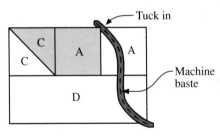

8. Now finish the unfinished seam in the third row, catching in the top end of the stem. Press.
9. Sew the first and second rows of the leaf together, and then sew them to the assembled third and fourth rows.

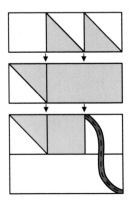

10. Hand sew the stem down along both edges, using an invisible appliqué stitch. Press. See the Lesson Box on page 24 for Freezer–Paper Appliqué.

Assembling the Quilt

Lay out your leaf blocks, alternating them with background blocks as in the illustration at the beginning of the chapter—or follow one of the quilts in the Gallery of Quilts (pages 9–14), or make up your own design. Move the leaves around until you like the distribution of colors. Sew the blocks together in rows and press the seams toward the background blocks. Then, sew the rows together and press the seams.

Add the inner border of background fabric, sides first and then the top and bottom. For detailed instructions, see Adding Borders, page 93.

For the pieced border, arrange the squares of leaf fabrics (Template A) around the edges of the quilt. Sew together 21 squares for each of the sides and press the seams all in the same direction. The finished strips should be the same length as the quilt top with its inner borders. Attach the side borders and press the seams.

Sew together 18 squares for the top border and 18 squares for the bottom border. Press the seams all in the same direction. Attach the top and bottom borders.

Quilting Suggestions

Draw long curling lines freehand, to suggest wind.

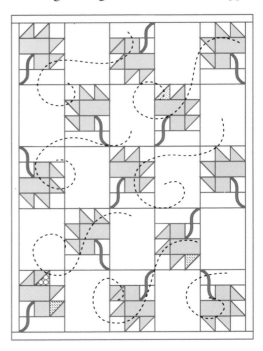

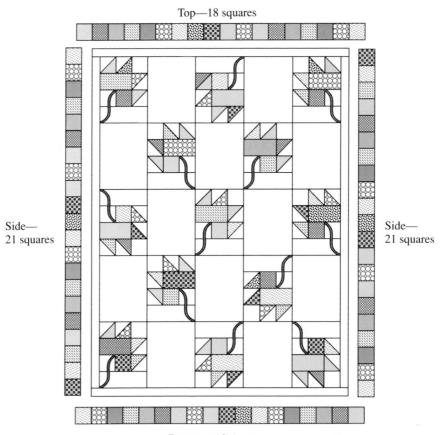

Top—18 squares

Side—21 squares

Side—21 squares

Bottom—18 squares

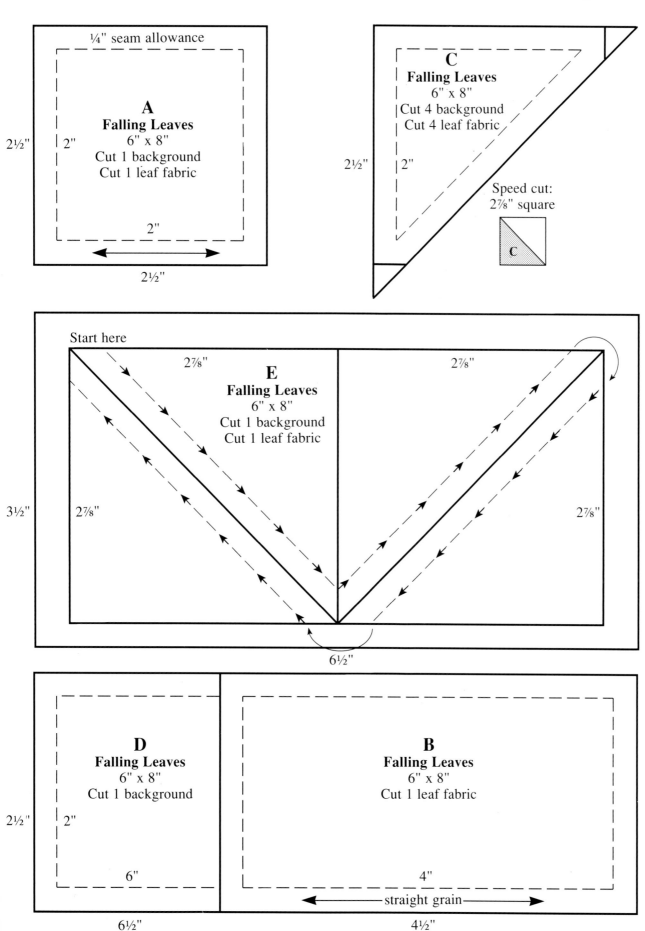

¼" seam allowance

A
Falling Leaves
6" x 8"
Cut 1 background
Cut 1 leaf fabric

2½"

2"

2"

2½"

C
Falling Leaves
6" x 8"
Cut 4 background
Cut 4 leaf fabric

2½"

2"

Speed cut:
2⅞" square

C

Start here

2⅞"

E
Falling Leaves
6" x 8"
Cut 1 background
Cut 1 leaf fabric

2⅞"

3½"

2⅞"

2⅞"

6½"

D
Falling Leaves
6" x 8"
Cut 1 background

2½"

2"

6"

6½"

B
Falling Leaves
6" x 8"
Cut 1 leaf fabric

4"

straight grain

4½"

November: Homespun Spools

Lessons
Prairie Points
Machine-Bartacked Buttons

This easy spool block is a good choice for a signature friendship quilt; I wrote the names of my "foremothers" on the squares. Prairie points are inserted between the inner and outer border strips. In place of quilting, old pearl buttons sewn on by machine hold the quilt together.

Quilt size: 36" x 42"
Block size: 6" x 6" (finished)
Number of blocks: 20 spool blocks

Fabric Required for Quilt Top
1½ yds. background
¼ yd. each of 10 plaid homespun fabrics
Also needed: about 100 assorted old buttons, and a colorfast marking pen if you want to write names on the blocks. Be sure to test your pen on your fabrics for colorfastness.

Cutting Instructions

Background
1. Make ten 2" cuts the width of the fabric, for blocks.
2. Make four 2½" cuts the width of the fabric, for the inner border.
3. Make four 4½" cuts the width of the fabric, for the outer border.

Plaid Fabrics
From each plaid homespun fabric, make one 2" cut the width of the fabric for blocks. Cut four squares 4" x 4" for prairie points.

Piecing Instructions
1. Sew a background strip to each strip of plaid homespun. Press each seam toward the plaid. Using Template A, cut 8 triangles from each set of strips as shown.

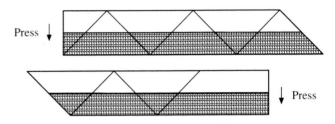

2. Assemble 4 triangles to make each spool block. Press triangles.

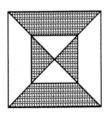

3. If you want signatures on your blocks, it is easiest to sign the blocks at this stage. Iron freezer paper onto the backs of the blocks to stabilize them and make them easier to write on. Peel the paper off before assembling the blocks.

Assembling the Quilt
1. Arrange the spools into 5 rows of 4 blocks each. Sew together in rows, then sew the rows to each other.

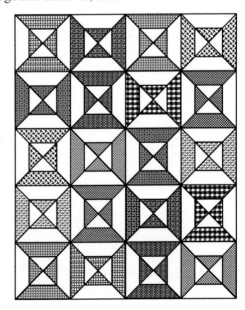

Homespun Spools *(November) by Joan Hanson, 1989, Seattle, Washington, 36" x 42". Old pearl buttons and homespun fabrics are reminiscent of pioneer times.*

Lesson Boxes—November

Prairie Points

Prairie points are made from folded squares of fabric. Fold each square diagonally. Fold again diagonally. This results in a triangle with all the raw edges together, along the longest side. Press.

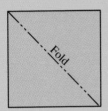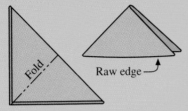

Arrange the prairie points around the edge of the quilt. Lay the raw edge of the prairie points along the raw edge of the quilt.

Lay the prairie points so that the final fold is always on the same side. Where the prairie points overlap, tuck the folded end of one inside the open end of the next.

Tuck each point between the folds
of the previous point

Baste the prairie points to the quilt, all the way around. Catch them in the seam and press them so they will lay on top of the outer border when it is added.

Machine-Bartacked Buttons

Lay out the quilt backing, batting, and top and pin baste the 3 layers together.

To attach the buttons, drop the feed dog on your sewing machine and set the stitch length at 0. Adjust the zigzag stitch width to match the holes in each button. Stitch the buttons on.

2. Add the 2½" strips to make the inner border, first to the sides and then to the top and bottom. Press.

3. Prepare 36 prairie points from 4" squares according to the directions in the Lesson Boxes. Baste them to the inner border, with 8 along the top and bottom edges and 10 on each side.

4. Sew on the outer border strips, first to the sides and then to the top and bottom. Press.

Quilting Suggestions

Rather than quilt this quilt, I like to bartack it with buttons at the center and the 4 corners of each spool. (See Machine-Bartacked Buttons in the Lesson Boxes.)

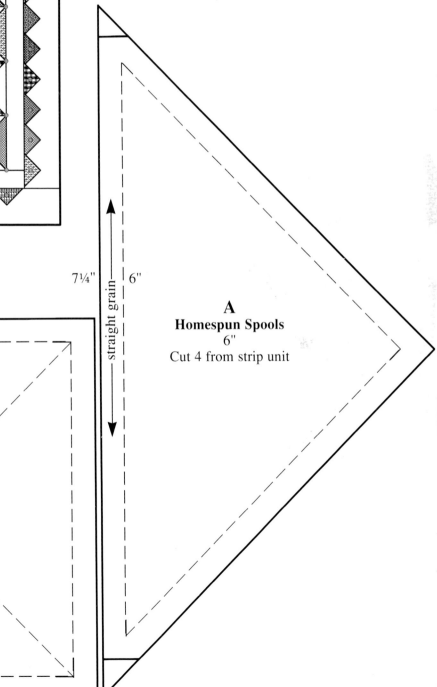

A
Homespun Spools
6"
Cut 4 from strip unit

7¼"   6"

straight grain

4"

¼" seam allowance

3½"

B
Homespun Spools
Prairie points
Cut 36

Fold

Fold

December: Hollyberry Star

Lesson
Mitering Corners

If you are tired of making the same kind of block over and over for a quilt, try a medallion quilt; make one large block for the center and work your way out from there. Try your hand at some appliquéd holly berries and leaves, or use the same space for a hand-quilted Christmas design.

Quilt size: 36" x 48"

Fabric Required for Quilt Top
½ yd. background
½ yd. dark red print
½ yd. green print
1½ yds. red solid
½ yd. purple solid
½ yd. holly print
green and red scraps for the holly leaves and berries

Cutting Instructions

Background
1. Cut 2 squares 9⅞" x 9⅞", then cut them in half diagonally.

2. Cut 4 squares 4½" x 4½" (Template D).
3. Cut 1 square 9¼" x 9¼", then cut it diagonally twice (or cut 4 of Template C).

Dark Red Print
1. Cut 1 square 6⅛" x 6⅛" (Template A).
2. Make 3 cuts, each 2½" wide, for checkerboard squares.

Green Print
1. Make 3 cuts, each 2½" wide, for checkerboard squares.
2. Cut 2 squares 4⅞" x 4⅞", then cut them in half diagonally. OR, cut 4 of Template B.

Red Solid
1. Make 2 cuts, each 2" wide, for border W; cut each in half to make 4 strips 2" x 21".
2. Cut 2 strips 4" x 50" and 2 strips 4" x 38" for outer border Z.

Purple Solid
Make 6 cuts, each 2" wide, for border Y. Cut 2 of the cuts to 38" and piece the others so you have two 50" strips.

Holly Print
1. Cut 8 strips, each 2½" x 15", for border X.
2. Cut 4 squares 4⅞" x 4⅞", then cut them in half diagonally (or cut 8 of Template B).

Green Scraps
Using appliqué template, cut 20 holly leaves, adding seam allowance.

Red Scraps
Using appliqué template, cut 20–25 circles for holly berries, adding seam allowance.

Piecing Instructions
1. Assemble the center star block by rows as shown below. Press.

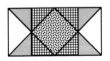

2. Add the 4 strips of red solid for border W, mitering the corners (see Lesson Box). The strips are oversized; trim the red border equally on all sides so that

Hollyberry Star *(December) by Joan Hanson, 1990, Seattle, Washington, 36" x 48". The gilded holly fabric and touch of purple provide an elegant holiday flair. Beautifully quilted by Hazel Montague.*

the block measures 18⅞" square. A handy way to do this is to use your 6" x 24" and 15" x 15" acrylic rulers side by side.

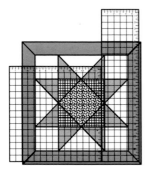

Trim to
18 ⅞"

3. Add the holly print for border X to the short sides of the large background triangles, mitering the corners. Use the Bias Square® to trim the ends of the border.

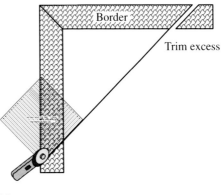

Border

Trim excess

Lesson Box—December

Mitering Corners

Using graph paper mounted on X-ray film or template plastic, make a guide to pinpoint the ¼" seam allowance on both sides of your corner. Punch a hole in 1 corner, ¼" in from both sides, with a ⅛" hole punch (available at office supply stores and a useful thing to have).

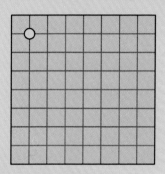

1/4" seam allowance guide for mitered and set-in corners

Use the guide to make a pencil mark on the wrong side of the fabric at all 4 corners.

Center the border strip on the side of the project, so that the strip extends an equal distance beyond each end of the block. Sew a ¼" seam, starting and ending ¼" in from the edge of the block and backstitching at both ends. Add the other 3 strips in the same manner.

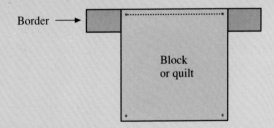

Border ⟶

Block or quilt

Using a 6" x 24" acrylic ruler with a 45° angle printed on it, mark a 45° angle on the wrong side of each strip, using your stitching line as a guide and starting at the intersection of the seam lines as shown.

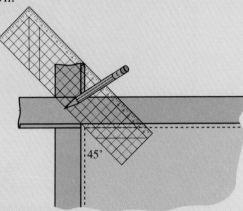

45°

Pin carefully, matching the marked lines, and sew along the lines. Backstitch at both ends.

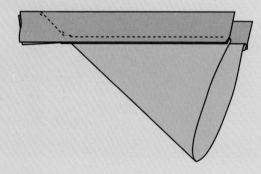

Trim seams to ¼" and press open.

4. Sew these 4 bordered triangles to the center square. Use the Bias Square to trim the ends of the border. The square should now measure 26½" x 26½".

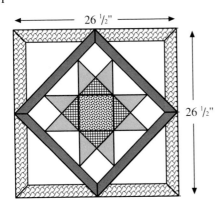

5. Appliqué on the holly berries and leaves, positioning them to your liking. (For appliqué instructions, see Lesson Boxes, pages 24–25.)

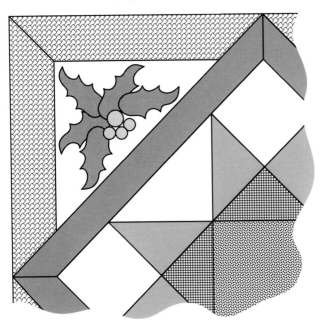

6. Strip piece the checkerboard section by making 2 sets of strips from the dark red print and green fabrics, as shown.

7. Press all seams toward the red fabric. From the set of strips with 2 red strips, make 14 crosscuts 2½" wide. From the set with 2 green strips, make 12 crosscuts 2½" wide.

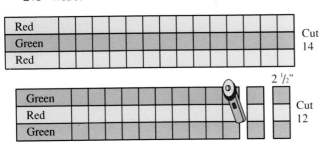

8. Assemble 2 rows of 13 crosscuts each, beginning and ending each row with a red crosscut. Press.

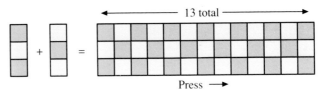

9. Sew the purple solid strips for border Y to the red solid strips for border Z. Press. Add the combined border strips to the quilt, mitering the corners.

Quilting Suggestions

Outline quilt the center star, holly berries and leaves, and inner border strips (see page 90). Quilt diagonally through the green squares of the checkerboard. Quilt holly leaves in the background of the star, and in the outer border. This holly-leaves border was adapted from Shirley Thompson's book *Old-Time Quilting Designs* and is fun to quilt because it is one continuous design.

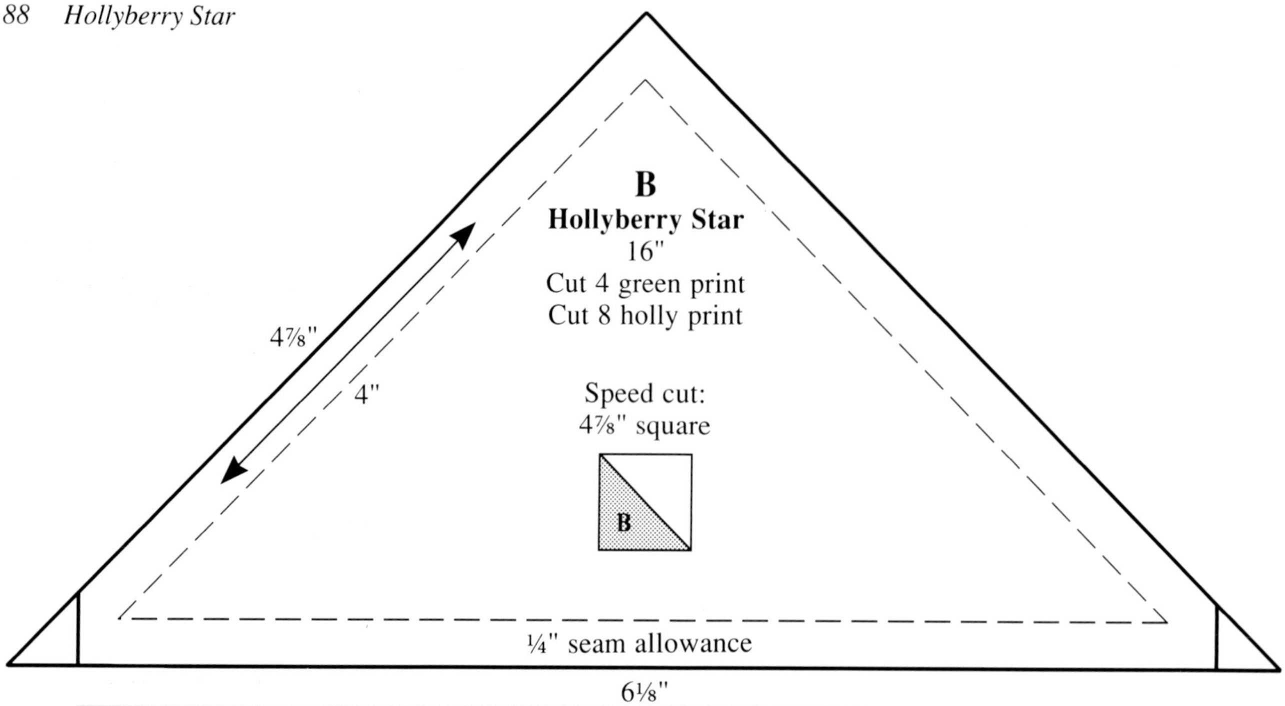

B
Hollyberry Star
16"
Cut 4 green print
Cut 8 holly print

Speed cut:
4⅞" square

B

4⅞"

4"

¼" seam allowance

6⅛"

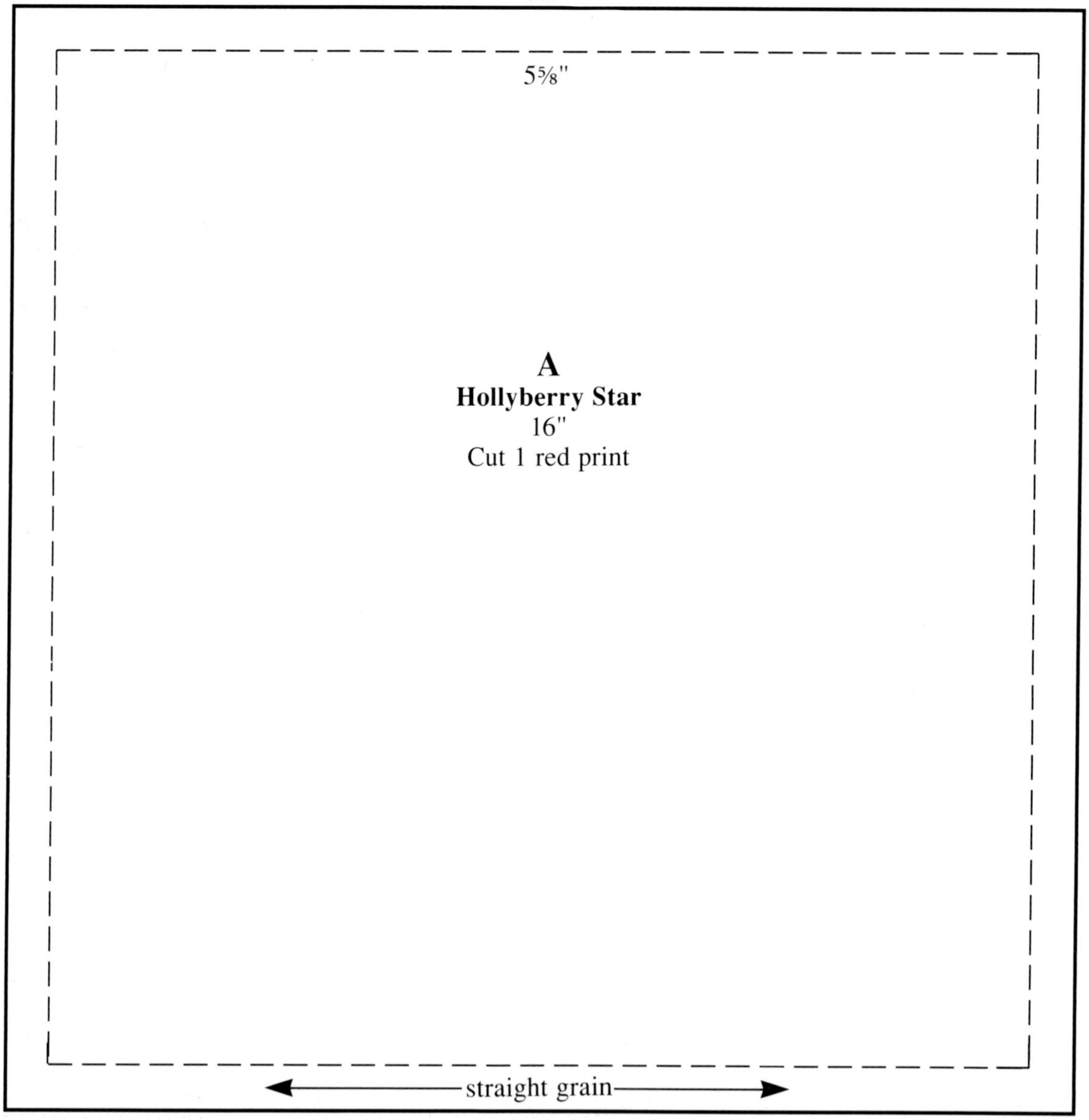

5⅝"

A
Hollyberry Star
16"
Cut 1 red print

← straight grain →

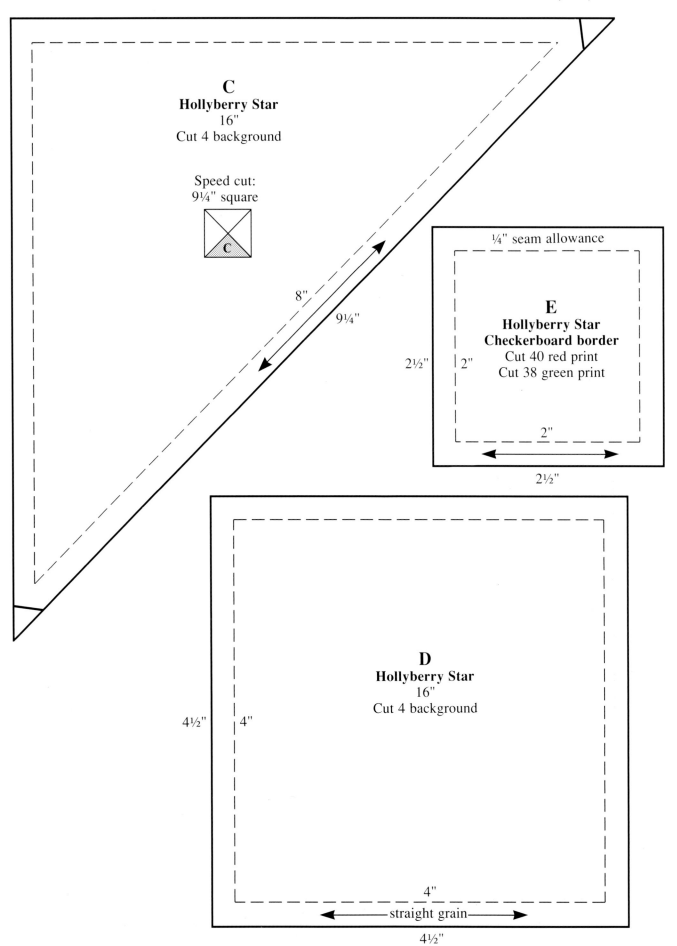

C
Hollyberry Star
16"
Cut 4 background

Speed cut:
9¼" square

C

8"

9¼"

¼" seam allowance

E
Hollyberry Star
Checkerboard border
Cut 40 red print
Cut 38 green print

2½"   2"

2"

2½"

D
Hollyberry Star
16"
Cut 4 background

4½"   4"

4"

straight grain

4½"

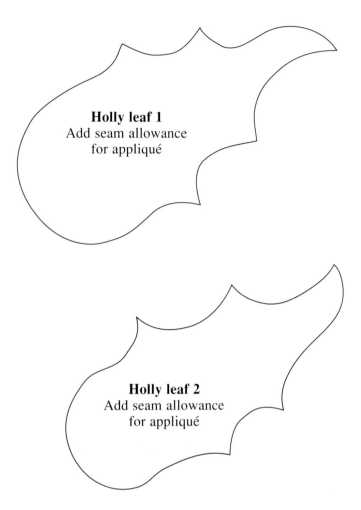

Holly leaf 1
Add seam allowance
for appliqué

Holly leaf 2
Add seam allowance
for appliqué

Make about 20 leaves total.
Reverse the direction of leaves
and use a variety of fabrics.

Holly berries

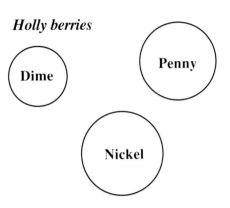

Dime

Penny

Nickel

Use templates or coins to trace
around, then add seam
allowance. Make about 7 of
each size in a variety of fabrics.

Start with
this end in
the corner

Quilting Design for Hollyberry Star

Design for
background of
star block

Finishing: From Tops to Quilts

Materials For Each Quilt

1¾ yds. fabric for quilt back and sleeve
(rod pocket)
⅓ to ½ yd. fabric for binding
40" x 50" piece of batting (Instead of buying crib-size
batts, buy a 90" x 108" size and cut it into quarters
for four quilts. Check the difference in cost!)
Be sure to prewash all fabrics before cutting.

Tools

12" or 15" acrylic square ruler
1" bias tape maker

Squaring Up Your Blocks

No matter how precisely you cut or how accurate your seam allowances are, the edges of your blocks may be a little off because of the stretch in the fabric. Trimming the edges will make it easier to join your blocks together.

A large acrylic ruler, 12" or 15" square, is very handy for squaring up your blocks. Place the ruler on top of your block. Line up the block with the grid lines on the ruler that correspond to the unfinished dimensions of the block. For example, if your block should be 10½" unfinished, line up the bottom and left edges of your block with the 10½" grid lines.

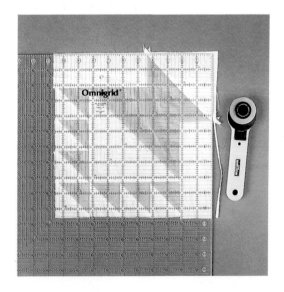

If your block is a little too large, it will extend beyond the top and right edges of the ruler. Center the block so that the excess is evenly distributed all the way around. With your rotary cutter, trim the excess off the right edge and the top edge. Lift off the ruler and turn the block so that the trimmed edges are now the left and bottom edges. Line up the grids on these trimmed edges, and trim any excess that extends beyond the right and top edges of the ruler.

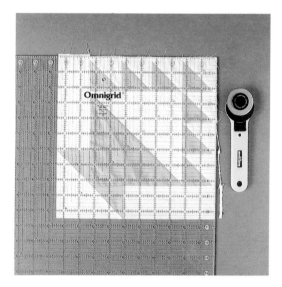

Before you trim, visualize where the ¼" seam line will be and consider what trimming will do to elements of your block design, such as the points of stars.

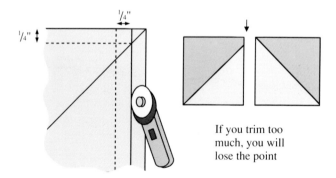

If you trim too much, you will lose the point

You might prefer to resew a few large blocks rather than cut into the design.

If your block is slightly too small, you may still be able to use it. A seam as narrow as ⅛" will hold on most 100% cotton fabrics, although it probably won't hold on a loosely woven fabric that frays. If a few of your blocks are slightly small, you may want to use your large square ruler to mark the seam line, so you will remember to take a narrower seam on these blocks. For example, if your block finishes at 10", center your block under the ruler and, using 10" as a guide, mark the stitching line.

Whatever is left over is the seam allowance.

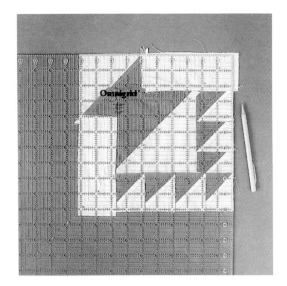

Adding Borders

With a few exceptions, the borders on these quilts are put on sides first, then the top and bottom. This order conserves fabric, since the side borders need be only as long as the body of the quilt, and not as long as the quilt including the top and bottom borders. If the borders are constructed this way, all four can be cut from the crosswise grain of the fabric; the 44" width of the fabric will be enough, and it won't be necessary to piece the border strips.

To determine the amount of fabric needed for the border of one of these quilts, multiply the width of the border (including seam allowances) by four. Cut the border strips selvage to selvage, so they are 44" to 45" long. Trim off the selvages.

Sew the side borders on and press the seams toward the borders. Trim the ends even with the top and bottom of the quilt.

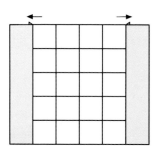

Sew on the top and bottom borders, press the seams toward the borders, and trim off the ends.

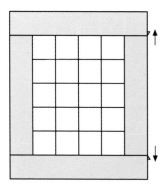

Marking Your Quilting Design

Wall quilts don't require as much quilting as quilts that receive a lot of heavy use, unless you would like to emphasize the quilting as I have in the May Baskets quilt and December's Hollyberry Star. Most of the quilts in this book are not heavily quilted.

You may prefer to mark the quilting lines on some of your quilts before basting them, while others can be marked as you go. Elaborate quilting designs should be marked before you sandwich the quilt, when it is easier to trace the quilting design accurately. Straight lines of quilting can usually be marked as you go, and in-the-ditch quilting will not need to be marked at all.

There are a variety of products available for marking quilts. Water-soluble pens are convenient, but be sure to test for removability on a scrap piece of your fabric before using the pen on your quilt. Dark fabrics can be marked with a chalk pencil or a sliver of soap. One-quarter-inch masking tape can be used to mark straight quilting lines.

If you mark the quilting design before you baste, you can trace your design onto all but the darkest fabrics. You will need a light source behind the design; either tape the design to a window and tape your quilt over it, or arrange a light table of sorts by supporting a piece of glass or Plexiglas over a small lamp. I do this by taking the leaf out of my dining room table and putting the glass or Plexiglas on top and a light below on a chair or on the floor. For dark fabrics, you may need to use a stencil and draw your quilting design on with chalk or soap.

Sandwiching Your Quilt

Combining the backing, the batting, and the quilt top is called sandwiching the quilt. If possible, both the backing and the batting should be about 2" larger than your quilt top.

To sandwich your quilt, press your backing fabric and lay it wrong side up on the floor or a low-loop carpet. Tape or pin down about every 8". Lay the batting on top of the backing and smooth it from the center out. Carefully lay the quilt on top, right side up, and pin it around the edges through all three layers.

If you are going to tie the quilt or machine quilt it, you can use safety pins to hold the three layers together instead of basting the layers with needle and thread. If you plan to hand quilt, baste the layers together. Use white thread and the 3"–5" long needles made for sewing soft-sculpture dolls. Take 2"–3" stitches. Baste diagonally from corner to corner to form an X, then back and forth in rows every 6" or so, starting from the center and working out to the edges.

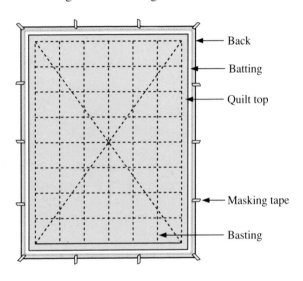

Back
Batting
Quilt top
Masking tape
Basting

Trim off excess batting, leaving about 1" all around. Save the leftover backing fabric to make the sleeve.

Quilting or Tying Your Quilt

If you would like to finish your quilt in less time than it would take to hand quilt it, there are several options: you can machine quilt it, tie it, or bartack it.

If you plan to machine quilt, you may want to safety-pin your quilt rather than baste it; basting stitches tend to catch on the machine's presser foot. Straight-line quilting and in-the-ditch quilting are easily done on the sewing machine.

When I tie quilts, I like to use embroidery floss. Ties should be 4"–6" apart. For a cleaner look, tie the knots on the back of the quilt.

Bartacking with a zigzag sewing machine is even

quicker than tying. Set your machine on the widest zigzag stitch, drop the feed dog, and make a bartack every 4"–6".

Making a Sleeve

If you are going to hang your quilt, you will want to attach a sleeve or rod pocket to the back. From the leftover backing fabric, cut a piece the width of your quilt (36") by 8". On each end, fold over ½" and then fold ½" again. Press.

½"   ½"

Stitch this hem. Fold the strip in half the long way, wrong sides together, and baste the raw edges to the top edge of the back of your quilt. Your quilt should be about 1" wider on both sides. This will be secured when you sew on the binding. Make a little pleat in the sleeve to accommodate the thickness of the rod, and then slip-stitch the bottom edge of the sleeve to the backing fabric.

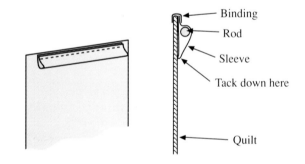

Binding
Rod
Sleeve
Tack down here
Quilt

Cut your hanging rod 1" shorter than the width of the quilt, so it will be hidden behind the quilt.

Binding Your Quilt

Everyone has a favorite way to bind a quilt; here's mine. I usually make bias binding because it wears better and looks smoother, but if I want to use a design such as a stripe in the fabric, or if I am short of fabric, I cut the binding on the straight of the grain. You will need about ⅓ yard of fabric if you cut the binding strips on the straight of the grain. You will need a little more fabric to make bias binding, about ½ yard.

For some quilts you may choose to use scraps 12" long or so, made of many of the fabrics used in the quilt.

This is the way I finished the March Irish Rose quilt.

To make bias binding, cut enough 2"-wide strips to go around the quilt and join them together with diagonal seams. Press the seams open.

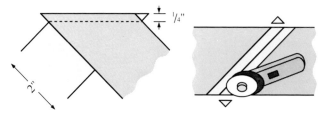

Feed your long bias strip through a bias tape maker, and press the two folds that the bias tape maker puts in.

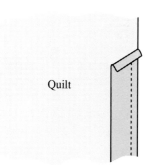

This gives you a strip of bias tape 1" wide, with ½" folded under on each edge.

Open up one edge of your strip and diagonally fold back the end. Starting at the center bottom of the quilt and using the ½" fold line as a sewing guide, stitch binding to quilt with a ½" seam.

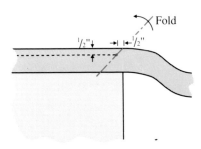

Quilt

Carefully feed the quilt and the binding through your machine at the same rate so that neither is stretched. Stop and backstitch ½" from the corner.

Fold

You may want to make a seam guide like the one described in the mitering Lesson Box on page 86, punching the hole ½" from both sides of the corners. This is a handy way to mark the back of your quilt so you know where to stop and backstitch the corners.

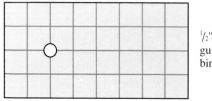

½" seam allowance guide for binding quilts

To begin the next side, fold the binding away from the quilt and then down so it is even with the next side.

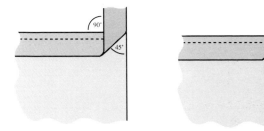

Start stitching at the edge, taking a ½" seam. Continue stitching around the quilt in the same manner.

When you get back to where you started, lap the end over the beginning and trim off the excess.

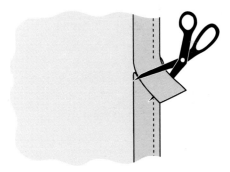

Fold the binding around to the back of the quilt and blindstitch it down, using the ½" fold line as a guide. A miter will form at each corner on the front. Fold each corner on the back as shown and stitch down.

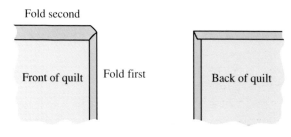

Fold second

Front of quilt   Fold first

Back of quilt